BIG BEND NATIONAL PARK

TRAVEL GUIDE 2024-2025

Explore Majestic Desert Landscapes, Hidden Trails, and Unforgettable Adventures in the Heart of Texas

Renee A. Gould

Map Of Big Bend National Park

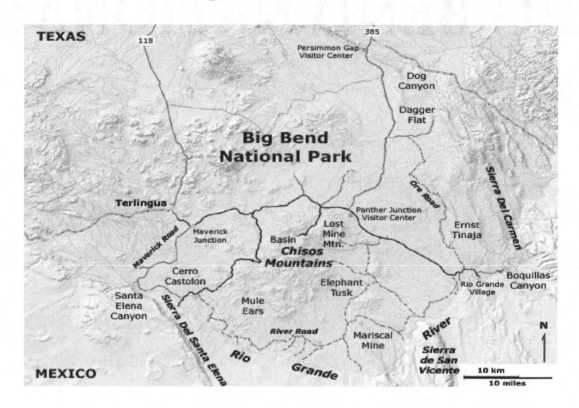

Rio Grande River With The United States On The Left And Mexico On The Right

Trail Along the Big Bend National Park

DISCLAIMER

This travel guide is provided for informational purposes only. The information contained herein is believed to be accurate and reliable as of the publication date, but may be subject to change. We are not making any warranty, express or implied, with respect to the content of this guide.

Users of this guide are responsible for verifying information independently and consulting appropriate authorities and resources prior to travel. We are not liable for any loss or damage caused by the reliance on information contained in this guide.

Information regarding travel advisories, visas, health, safety, and other important considerations can change rapidly. Users are advised to check for the most up-to-date information from official government and travel industry sources before embarking on any trip.

Travel inherently involves risk, and users are responsible for making their own informed decisions and accepting any associated risks.

Table Of Content

1. Introduction

1.1 Overview of Big Bend National Park

Big Bend National Park is a spectacular area located in the far west of Texas, near the border with Mexico. It is a place where the beauty of nature meets a rich history, making it one of the most unique national parks in the United States. Established in 1944, the park covers over 800,000 acres, which is larger than the state of Rhode Island. It was named after the "bend" in the Rio Grande River, which winds through the landscape and forms part of the international boundary between the United States and Mexico.

A Diverse Landscape

The park is known for its incredible diversity in landscapes. Here, you will find towering mountains, sprawling deserts, deep canyons, and the flowing waters of the Rio Grande. Each part of the park offers a different experience:

Mountains: The Chisos Mountains rise dramatically in the center of the park, providing breathtaking views and cooler temperatures. These mountains are home to a variety of wildlife and unique plants that thrive at higher elevations.

Deserts: The surrounding desert is filled with fascinating plant life, including cacti and wildflowers that bloom in the spring. The desert landscape is stark yet beautiful, with vast stretches of open land that create a sense of solitude and peace.

Rivers: The Rio Grande runs along the park's southern edge, creating stunning canyons like Santa Elena Canyon, where the cliffs tower high above the river. This river not only serves as a natural border but also offers recreational opportunities such as canoeing, kayaking, and fishing.

Rich Biodiversity

Big Bend is not just about stunning scenery; it is also a haven for wildlife. The park is home to over 450 species of birds, making it a prime location for birdwatching. You might see everything from colorful songbirds to majestic hawks. Additionally, there are numerous mammals, reptiles, and insects that thrive in the various ecosystems found within the park. Visitors may encounter deer, coyotes, javelinas, and even the elusive mountain lion if they're lucky.

Cultural and Historical Significance

The history of Big Bend is as rich as its landscapes. The area has been inhabited for thousands of years, with evidence of Native American tribes such as the Chisos and the Mescalero Apache who once lived here. You can still see traces of their culture, including ancient rock art found in some remote areas of the park.

In the late 19th and early 20th centuries, settlers moved into the region, and remnants of their lives can still be found today. For instance, you can explore the old ruins of a ranch or visit the historic towns nearby, where stories of the past come to life.

Outdoor Activities

Big Bend National Park is a paradise for those who love outdoor activities. Here are some of the popular things you can do:

Hiking: With over 150 miles of hiking trails, there are paths for everyone, from easy walks to challenging hikes. Some trails lead to stunning overlooks, while others take you deep into the wilderness.

Camping: There are several campgrounds within the park where you can spend the night under the stars. For those seeking solitude, backcountry camping allows you to truly immerse yourself in nature.

Wildlife Watching: Whether you're interested in birds or larger mammals, there are plenty of opportunities to observe wildlife. Early morning or late afternoon are the best times to spot animals when they are most active.

Stargazing: Due to its remote location, Big Bend is one of the best places in the country for stargazing. The night sky is filled with countless stars, and many visitors enjoy attending special astronomy events hosted by the park.

Planning Your Visit

Planning a trip to Big Bend can be an adventure in itself. The park's remote location means that it is not as crowded as other national parks, providing a more peaceful experience. However, it's important to prepare ahead of time. Understanding the best times to visit, what to pack, and the available amenities will help you make the most of your trip.

In this guide, we aim to provide you with all the information you need to explore Big Bend National Park fully. From practical tips on how to plan your visit to detailed descriptions of hiking trails, campsites, and wildlife watching spots, you'll find everything you need to make your adventure memorable. Get ready to discover one of America's hidden gems, where nature's beauty and rich history await you!

1.2 Importance of the Park in Conservation and Recreation

Big Bend National Park plays a crucial role in both conservation efforts and recreational opportunities. Its vast landscapes and diverse ecosystems make it a key area for protecting wildlife, preserving natural habitats, and providing a space for people to connect with nature. Here's a closer look at the park's importance in these two areas:

1. Conservation Efforts

Biodiversity Preservation: Big Bend is home to a wide range of plant and animal species, many of which are found nowhere else in the world. By designating this area as a national park, we help protect these species and their habitats from urban development, pollution, and other human activities that threaten their survival.

Ecosystem Protection: The park encompasses several distinct ecosystems, including desert, river, and mountainous environments. Each of these ecosystems supports different forms of life. By conserving these varied habitats, Big Bend plays a vital role in maintaining ecological balance and promoting biodiversity.

Research and Education: The park serves as a natural laboratory for scientists and researchers studying climate change, geology, and ecology. It offers valuable insights into how different ecosystems function and how they may adapt to environmental changes. Educational programs for visitors promote awareness about the importance of conservation and inspire future generations to protect these natural resources.

Cultural Preservation: The park also safeguards important cultural and historical sites, protecting the stories of the Native American tribes and early settlers who inhabited the region. This preservation ensures that future generations can learn from and appreciate the rich history that shapes the area.

2. Recreation Opportunities

Outdoor Activities: Big Bend offers a plethora of outdoor activities for visitors of all interests and skill levels. From hiking and camping to canoeing and stargazing, there is something for everyone. The park's extensive trail system invites hikers to explore its stunning landscapes, while the river provides opportunities for water-based recreation.

Escape from Urban Life: The remote location of Big Bend allows visitors to disconnect from the hustle and bustle of daily life. Its vast open spaces provide a serene environment where people can relax, reflect, and rejuvenate. Whether it's sitting by the river, hiking in the mountains, or camping under a blanket of stars, the park encourages visitors to immerse themselves in nature.

Connecting with Nature: Recreation in Big Bend promotes a deeper appreciation for the natural world. As people engage in outdoor activities, they often develop a stronger connection to the environment. This connection can inspire individuals to become advocates for conservation and environmental protection.

Community and Education: The park hosts various programs, events, and workshops that bring together visitors and locals. These activities not only enhance the recreational experience but also foster a sense of community and shared purpose in protecting the park's natural resources.

3. Conclusion

In summary, Big Bend National Park is vital for conservation and recreation. Its protection of unique ecosystems and wildlife contributes significantly to global biodiversity efforts. At the same time, the park provides countless opportunities for people to engage with nature, escape from everyday life, and develop a deeper understanding of the environment. By balancing conservation with recreation, Big Bend National Park stands as a testament to the importance of preserving our natural heritage for future generations.

1.3 Key Facts and Figures

Understanding the essential facts and figures about Big Bend National Park can enhance your appreciation of this remarkable place. Here are some key details that highlight the park's size, diversity, and significance:

1. Location

State: Texas

Region: Far West Texas, near the Mexico border

Nearest Towns: Terlingua and Study Butte are the closest communities, providing access to services and accommodations.

2. Size and Area

Total Area: Approximately 800,000 acres (1,200 square miles), making it one of the largest national parks in the United States.

Elevation Range: The park's elevation varies significantly, ranging from about 1,800 feet (550 meters) at the Rio Grande to over 7,800 feet (2,400 meters) at the top of Emory Peak.

3. Geography

Major Landforms: The park features the Chisos Mountains, the Rio Grande River, and expansive desert plains. The Chisos Mountains are unique as they are the only mountain range entirely contained within a national park in Texas.

Notable Canyons: Santa Elena Canyon, Boquillas Canyon, and Mariscal Canyon are prominent canyons carved by the Rio Grande, showcasing dramatic cliffs and stunning views.

4. Flora and Fauna

Plant Species: The park is home to over 1,200 plant species, including cacti, wildflowers, and various trees adapted to arid conditions.

Wildlife: Big Bend hosts more than 450 species of birds, 75 species of mammals, and numerous reptiles and amphibians. This diversity includes unique species like the black-tailed rattlesnake and the endangered Texas horned lizard.

5. Climate

Temperature Range: The climate varies greatly due to the elevation changes. Summer temperatures can soar above 100°F (38°C) in the lower elevations, while winter temperatures can drop below freezing at higher altitudes.

Rainfall: The park receives an average of 10 to 25 inches (25 to 63 cm) of rainfall per year, with most precipitation occurring during the summer months.

6. Visitors

Annual Attendance: Big Bend National Park sees approximately 400,000 visitors each year, with the peak season occurring from late fall to early spring when the weather is milder.

Visitor Demographics: The park attracts a diverse range of visitors, including families, outdoor enthusiasts, and international travelers, offering programs and facilities to cater to various interests.

7. Recreational Opportunities

Hiking Trails: The park features over 150 miles of hiking trails, ranging from easy walks to challenging hikes, including popular trails like the Lost Mine Trail and the Window Trail.

Camping: There are several campgrounds within the park, including designated sites and backcountry camping options. Reservations are recommended during peak seasons.

Scenic Drives: Visitors can enjoy scenic drives such as the Ross Maxwell Scenic Drive, which offers breathtaking views and access to several trailheads and viewpoints.

8. Cultural and Historical Significance

Archeological Sites: Evidence of human activity in the area dates back over 9,000 years, with numerous archeological sites showcasing the history of Native American tribes and early settlers.

Historic Structures: The park features several historic buildings, including the Castolon Historic District, which offers insights into the lives of early settlers and the region's history.

These key facts and figures illustrate the remarkable features of Big Bend National Park. From its vast landscapes and rich biodiversity to its cultural history and recreational opportunities, the park is a significant natural treasure worth exploring. Understanding these aspects will help you appreciate the beauty and complexity of this unique destination as you plan your visit.

2. Planning Your Visit

2.1 Best Times to Visit

Choosing the right time to visit Big Bend National Park can greatly enhance your experience, allowing you to enjoy the park's beauty and activities to the fullest. The park's unique climate and geographical features create distinct seasonal changes, so here's a breakdown of what to expect during each season:

1. Spring (March to May)

Weather: Spring is one of the most popular times to visit Big Bend. Temperatures start to warm up, with daytime highs ranging from the mid-70s to mid-90s °F (around 24 to 35 °C). Nights can still be cool, especially in March and April.

Wildflowers: This season often brings beautiful wildflower blooms, especially in March and April. Visitors can enjoy vibrant displays of color throughout the park.

Activities: Spring is ideal for hiking, camping, and wildlife watching. Animals become more active as temperatures rise, and migratory birds return, making it a great time for birdwatching.

Crowds: Spring break and weekends can be busy, so plan ahead for accommodations and trails.

2. Summer (June to August)

Weather: Summer in Big Bend can be extremely hot, with daytime temperatures often exceeding 100 °F (38 °C) in lower elevations. The heat can be intense, especially in July and August.

Activities: Early mornings and late afternoons are the best times for outdoor activities to avoid the hottest parts of the day. Nighttime offers cooler temperatures and excellent stargazing opportunities.

Crowds: This season tends to be less crowded, especially in late summer. Many visitors choose to avoid the heat, but those who do come can enjoy a more solitary experience.

Rainfall: Brief rain showers can occur, especially during monsoon season in late July and August, which can bring some relief from the heat.

3. Fall (September to November)

Weather: Fall offers a gradual cooling down from the summer heat. September can still be quite warm, with temperatures starting to drop significantly in October and November, reaching daytime highs in the 70s and 80s °F (21 to 29 °C).

Scenic Views: Fall foliage can be seen, particularly in the Chisos Mountains, providing beautiful views against the desert backdrop.

Activities: This season is great for hiking and camping, as the weather is generally pleasant and comfortable. Wildlife activity also picks up as animals prepare for winter.

Crowds: Fall is a popular time for visitors, especially during the Thanksgiving holiday, so it's wise to make reservations in advance.

4. Winter (December to February)

Weather: Winter is the least crowded season at Big Bend. Daytime temperatures can range from the upper 50s to mid-70s °F (around 15 to 24 °C), but nights can be cold, sometimes dropping below freezing.

Activities: This is a fantastic time for those who enjoy hiking without the heat and want to experience solitude in nature. The cooler weather allows for longer hikes and comfortable camping.

Wildlife: Many animals are more active in the cooler weather, and it's a great time for birdwatching, especially for species that migrate south for the winter.

Crowds: Expect fewer crowds during winter, making it easier to explore popular sites and enjoy the peace of the park.

Conclusion

In summary, the best time to visit Big Bend National Park depends on your preferences for weather, activities, and crowd levels. Spring and fall offer pleasant temperatures and vibrant scenery, while summer can be very hot but offers solitude and stargazing opportunities. Winter brings cool weather and fewer visitors, allowing for a peaceful retreat. Regardless of when you choose to visit, Big Bend's stunning landscapes and diverse wildlife promise an unforgettable experience. Be sure to plan accordingly based on the season and what activities you wish to enjoy!

2.2 Park Accessibility and Entrance Fees

Understanding the accessibility of Big Bend National Park and the associated entrance fees is essential for planning a smooth visit. Here's what you need to know about getting to the park and the costs involved.

1. Park Accessibility

Location and Access Points:
Big Bend National Park is located in a remote area of West Texas, making it less accessible than some other national parks. The nearest major city is El Paso, which is about 200 miles (322 kilometers) to the northwest. The closest towns, Terlingua and Study Butte, are located just outside the park's boundaries, providing essential services like gas, groceries, and accommodations.

Driving Directions:
The most common way to access the park is by car. Here are the main routes:

From the West: Take Highway 90 to Marathon, then turn onto Highway 385 south, which leads directly to the park's entrance.

From the East: Traveling from Fort Stockton, take Highway 285 south to Highway 90, and then follow Highway 90 west to Highway 385.

From the South: Visitors coming from Mexico can enter through the Boquillas Crossing, which allows access to the park from the Mexican town of Boquillas del Carmen. A valid passport is required for crossing the border.

Public Transportation:
Public transportation options to the park are limited due to its remote location. Some visitors may find tour services or shuttles available from nearby towns, but renting a car is often the most convenient option.

Accessibility for All Visitors:
Big Bend National Park strives to be accessible to all visitors. While many of the park's remote areas may require hiking, there are accessible facilities, including:

Visitor Center: The Panther Junction Visitor Center has accessible restrooms and exhibit areas.

Accessible Trails: Some trails, such as the Chisos Basin Trail and the short walk to the Rio Grande, offer accessible paths suitable for wheelchairs and strollers.

2. Entrance Fees

Big Bend National Park requires an entrance fee, which helps fund park maintenance and visitor services. Here's a breakdown of the current fees:

Standard Entrance Fee:

>   **Private Vehicle:** $30 for a 7-day pass. This fee covers all passengers in a single, private vehicle.

>   **Motorcycle:** $25 for a 7-day pass.

>   **Pedestrians/Bicyclists:** $15 per person for a 7-day pass.

Annual Pass:

>   For those who plan to visit multiple times within a year, the Big Bend Annual Pass is available for $55. This pass allows unlimited entry to the park for one year from the date of purchase.

Interagency Passes:

If you hold a National Parks pass (like the America the Beautiful Pass), it provides free entrance to the park. This pass can be a cost-effective option for frequent national park visitors.

Fees for Special Programs:

Some ranger-led programs, guided tours, or special events may have additional fees. It's best to check the park's official website or contact the visitor center for details on any specific programs.

Payment Options:

Entrance fees can be paid at the park entrance stations, and most major credit cards are accepted. It's also possible to pay online in advance through the National Park Service website.

Knowing how to access Big Bend National Park and understanding the entrance fees will help you plan a successful visit. With its breathtaking landscapes and outdoor activities, the park is well worth the trip. Be sure to check the park's official website for the most current information on accessibility, fees, and any potential changes that may occur before your visit. Whether you're driving through or planning an extended stay, Big Bend has something for everyone to enjoy.

2.3 What to Pack: Essentials and Recommendations

Packing the right gear is crucial for enjoying your visit to Big Bend National Park. The park's diverse landscapes, varying elevations, and changing weather conditions require thoughtful preparation. Here's a comprehensive list of essentials and recommendations to ensure a safe and enjoyable experience.

1. Clothing Essentials

Layered Clothing:
Temperatures can fluctuate dramatically throughout the day, especially between high elevations and desert areas. Dressing in layers allows you to adapt to changing conditions. Consider the following:

> **Base Layer:** Lightweight moisture-wicking shirts and pants to keep you comfortable and dry.

> **Insulating Layer:** A fleece or lightweight jacket for cooler mornings and evenings.

> **Outer Layer:** A waterproof and windproof jacket to protect against rain and wind.

Hiking Pants/Shorts:
Choose breathable, quick-drying fabrics. If you're planning on hiking, wear pants or shorts with a good range of motion.

Hiking Boots or Shoes:
Comfortable, sturdy footwear is essential. Waterproof hiking boots are recommended, especially if you plan to explore rocky or uneven terrain.

Hat and Sunglasses:
A wide-brimmed hat provides shade and protection from the sun, while UV-blocking sunglasses will help protect your eyes from harsh sunlight.

Swimwear:
If you plan to enjoy the Rio Grande or any swimming areas, pack a swimsuit.

2. Hydration and Nutrition

Water:
Staying hydrated is vital, especially in the hot and dry climate. Bring a reusable water bottle or hydration reservoir with at least 2 liters (68 ounces) of water per person per day.

Snacks:
Pack high-energy snacks, such as granola bars, nuts, dried fruit, or trail mix, to keep your energy levels up while exploring.

3. Navigation and Safety Gear

Map and Compass:
Even though many trails are well-marked, having a physical map and compass is a good idea, as cell service can be limited.

First Aid Kit:
A basic first aid kit should include band-aids, antiseptic wipes, pain relievers, and any personal medications.

Multi-Tool or Knife:
A multi-tool can be handy for various situations, from opening food packages to minor repairs.

4. Camping Gear (if applicable)

Tent:
Choose a weather-appropriate tent that is easy to set up and provides good protection against the elements.

Sleeping Bag and Pad:
A sleeping bag rated for cooler temperatures, along with a sleeping pad for comfort and insulation from the ground.

Camp Stove or Cooking Gear:
If you plan to cook, pack a portable stove and cooking utensils. Don't forget fuel!

Food:
Bring enough food for your stay, focusing on lightweight and non-perishable items.

5. Wildlife and Environmental Considerations

Binoculars:
A good pair of binoculars is excellent for wildlife watching and enjoying the stunning vistas from overlooks.

Insect Repellent:
Depending on the time of year, you may encounter insects. Use a DEET-based insect repellent to keep bugs at bay.

Sunscreen:

Protect your skin from harmful UV rays with broad-spectrum sunscreen, even on cloudy days.

6. Photography Gear

Camera:

Bring a camera or smartphone to capture the breathtaking landscapes and wildlife. A lightweight tripod can help with stability, especially in low-light conditions.

Extra Batteries and Memory Cards:

Ensure you have enough power and storage for all your photos.

7. Personal Items

Toiletries:

Bring personal hygiene items, including toothbrush, toothpaste, and biodegradable soap if you plan to camp.

Trash Bags:

Carry out what you bring in. Leave No Trace principles are essential for preserving the natural beauty of the park.

Packing thoughtfully for your trip to Big Bend National Park will enhance your experience and ensure you're prepared for the varying conditions. Remember to check the weather forecast before your trip, and adjust your packing list accordingly. By bringing the right gear, you'll be ready to explore all that this beautiful park has to offer, from hiking the trails to relaxing under the stars. Enjoy your adventure!

2.4 Safety Tips and Guidelines

Safety should always be a priority when visiting Big Bend National Park. The park's remote location, diverse terrain, and varying weather conditions require visitors to be prepared and aware of their surroundings. Here are some essential safety tips and guidelines to help you have a safe and enjoyable experience in the park.

1. Stay Hydrated

Drink Plenty of Water:
The dry desert climate can lead to dehydration quickly, especially during warmer months.

Aim to drink at least 2 liters (68 ounces) of water per person per day, and increase your intake during strenuous activities.

Recognize Signs of Dehydration:
Be aware of symptoms such as dry mouth, dizziness, and fatigue. If you notice these signs, take a break, find shade, and drink water immediately.

2. Be Prepared for Weather Changes

Check the Forecast:
Before heading out, check the weather forecast for the day and upcoming days. Big Bend can experience sudden changes in weather, especially in higher elevations.

Dress in Layers:
As temperatures can vary significantly throughout the day, wear layered clothing that can be easily added or removed as conditions change.

3. Stay on Designated Trails

Follow Park Guidelines:
To minimize your impact on the environment and for your safety, always stick to marked trails. Venturing off-trail can damage delicate ecosystems and increase your risk of getting lost.

Be Cautious on Slippery Terrain:
Some trails can be steep or rocky. Take your time, watch your footing, and use trekking poles if needed for stability.

4. Wildlife Safety

Keep a Safe Distance:
Observe wildlife from a safe distance, at least 100 yards (91 meters) from large animals like bears and bison, and at least 25 yards (23 meters) from smaller animals. Never approach or feed wildlife, as this can be dangerous for both you and the animals.

Store Food Properly:
If camping, store food and scented items in bear-proof containers or hang them from trees to prevent attracting wildlife.

5. Be Aware of the Environment

Watch for Cacti and Thorns:
The park is home to various cacti and thorny plants. Be cautious while hiking and avoid brushing against vegetation.

Sun Protection:
Use sunscreen, sunglasses, and hats to protect yourself from the sun's harmful rays, even on cloudy days.

6. Be Prepared for Emergencies

First Aid Kit:
Carry a basic first aid kit for minor injuries. Familiarize yourself with its contents and how to use them.

Know Emergency Contacts:
Familiarize yourself with the park's emergency contact information and locate the nearest visitor center or ranger station in case you need assistance.

7. Hiking Safety

Inform Someone of Your Plans:
Always let someone know your hiking plans, including your expected return time. This is especially important if you are going solo or hiking in remote areas.

Know Your Limits:
Choose trails that match your fitness level and experience. If you're feeling fatigued, it's best to turn back rather than push yourself.

Start Early:
For longer hikes, start early in the day to avoid hiking during the hottest part of the day. This is also crucial if you're hiking to higher elevations where temperatures drop quickly at night.

8. Nighttime Safety

Stargazing Precautions:
If you plan to stargaze or hike at night, use a flashlight or headlamp with a red filter to preserve your night vision. Always stay on trails and be aware of your surroundings.

Check for Wildlife Activity:
Be mindful of nocturnal wildlife. Animals are often more active at night, so stay alert while exploring.

By following these safety tips and guidelines, you can ensure a safe and enjoyable visit to Big Bend National Park. Preparation and awareness are key to navigating the park's beautiful but sometimes challenging environment. With the right precautions in place, you can fully immerse yourself in the park's stunning landscapes and diverse wildlife while having a memorable outdoor adventure. Enjoy your time in this breathtaking natural wonder!

3. Getting There

3.1 Transportation Options

Getting to Big Bend National Park requires some planning due to its remote location in West Texas. Below are the main transportation options to help you reach the park, including details about pricing and logistics.

3.1.1 By Car

Driving is the most common and convenient way to get to Big Bend National Park. The park is located approximately 200 miles (322 kilometers) from El Paso, the nearest major city. Here's what you need to know about driving to the park:

Main Highways:
The primary routes to the park are:

From the West: Take U.S. Highway 90 to Marathon, then head south on Highway 385 directly to the park entrance.

From the East: If traveling from Fort Stockton, take Highway 285 south to Highway 90, then west to Highway 385.

From the South: Visitors coming from Mexico can cross into the U.S. at the Boquillas Crossing. A valid passport is required, and the border crossing hours may vary, so check in advance.

Driving Times:
Here are estimated driving times from major cities:

El Paso to Big Bend: About 3.5 to 4 hours (200 miles)

Marathon to Big Bend: Approximately 30 minutes (30 miles)

Fort Stockton to Big Bend: About 1.5 hours (90 miles)

Road Conditions:
Most roads leading to the park are paved and well-maintained. However, some backroads may be unpaved, so a high-clearance vehicle may be necessary if you plan to explore remote areas.

Fuel Availability:
Fuel stations are limited within the park. The nearest gas stations are located in the nearby towns of Terlingua and Study Butte. It's advisable to fill up your tank before entering the park and to keep an eye on your fuel levels while exploring.

Cost Considerations:

Fuel Costs: Average gas prices in West Texas can vary, but expect to pay around $3.50 to $4.00 per gallon. Calculate your estimated mileage to budget for fuel.

3.1.2 By Air

Flying is another option for reaching Big Bend National Park, especially if you're coming from outside Texas or from far away. Here's how to get to the park by air:

Nearest Airports:
The nearest major airports to Big Bend are:

> **El Paso International Airport (ELP):** About 200 miles (322 kilometers) from the park. This airport offers various domestic flights and some international options.

> **Midland International Air and Space Port (MAF):** Approximately 170 miles (274 kilometers) away. Similar to El Paso, this airport offers multiple domestic flights.

> **Alpine-Casparis Municipal Airport (E38):** This is a smaller regional airport located about 90 miles (145 kilometers) from the park. It has limited flight options and is mainly used for general aviation.

Car Rentals:
Upon arriving at the airport, renting a car is the best option for getting to Big Bend. Most major car rental companies operate at both El Paso and Midland airports. Rental prices can vary widely, but expect to pay around $40 to $100 per day, depending on the vehicle type and rental company.

Travel Time:
From El Paso, it will take approximately 3.5 to 4 hours to drive to Big Bend National Park. From Midland, the drive will take about 2.5 to 3 hours.

Cost Considerations:

Airfare: Prices for flights can vary significantly based on your departure city, the time of year, and how far in advance you book. On average, round-trip domestic flights to El Paso or Midland can range from $150 to $500 or more.

Rental Car Costs: In addition to rental fees, consider insurance options, gas costs, and any additional fees for drop-off at different locations.

3.1.3 Public Transportation

Public transportation options to Big Bend National Park are quite limited due to its remote location. However, here are some options you might consider:

Bus Services:

> **Greyhound:** The Greyhound bus service has routes that connect to nearby towns like Alpine or Fort Stockton. However, these routes may require multiple transfers and could take a significant amount of time. From Alpine or Fort Stockton, you would need to arrange a taxi or rideshare to reach the park.
>
> **Approximate Cost:** Greyhound fares can vary, but expect to pay around $30 to $100 for a one-way ticket, depending on the distance and route.

Shuttle Services:
Some local companies may offer shuttle services to and from the park. These services are often limited and may need to be booked in advance. Contact local tourism offices in Alpine or Terlingua for more information about available shuttles.

Tours:
Some tour companies provide guided trips from cities like El Paso or Austin to Big Bend. These tours can include transportation, park entrance fees, and guided hikes, but they often come at a premium price.

> **Approximate Cost:** Tour prices can range from $100 to $300 per person, depending on the length and inclusions of the tour.

Conclusion

Getting to Big Bend National Park involves careful planning, especially given its remote location. Whether you choose to drive, fly, or use public transportation, understanding your options and associated costs will help you prepare for your trip. Regardless of your choice, the journey to Big Bend is well worth it for the breathtaking landscapes and outdoor adventures that await you.

3.2 Nearby Towns and Accommodations

When visiting Big Bend National Park, it's essential to know about nearby towns where you can find accommodations, dining, and other amenities. The park is remote, so planning your stay in these towns will make your visit more comfortable. Here's a detailed look at the main towns near Big Bend, including accommodation options, addresses, contact information, and approximate pricing.

1. Terlingua

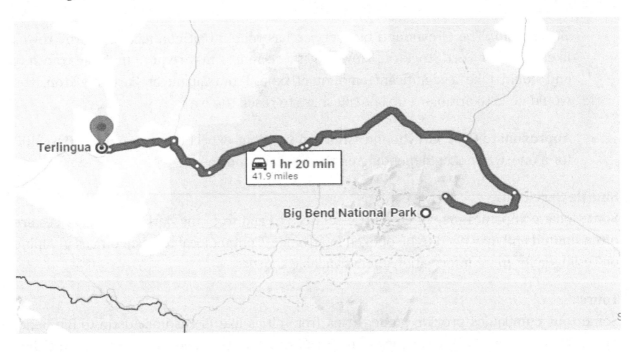

Overview:

Terlingua is the closest town to Big Bend National Park, located about 15 miles (24 kilometers) from the park's entrance. Known for its ghost town and vibrant arts community, Terlingua offers a variety of accommodations, from rustic cabins to hotels.

Accommodations:

Chisos Mountains Lodge

    Address: Big Bend National Park, TX 79834

    Contact: (432) 477-2291

    Website: https://www.chisosmountainslodge.com

    Price: $120 to $250 per night (varies by season and room type)

    Description: Located within the park, this lodge offers comfortable rooms and a restaurant with stunning mountain views. It's an excellent base for exploring the park.

Terlingua Ranch Lodge

    Address: 1 Terlingua Ranch Rd, Terlingua, TX 79852

    Contact: (432) 371-3382

    Website: https://www.terlinguaranch.com

    Price: $90 to $150 per night (varies by room type)

    Description: Set in a beautiful location, this lodge provides a range of accommodations, including rooms, RV sites, and tent camping. It features a restaurant and offers guided tours of the area.

The Starlight Theatre

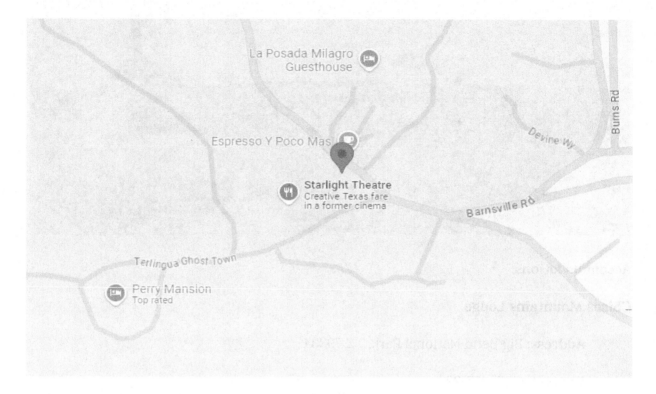

Address: 109 Starlight Theatre Rd, Terlingua, TX 79852

Contact: (432) 371-2326

Website: http://www.starlighttheatre.com

Price: $75 to $150 per night (varies by room type)

Description: This historic theater turned hotel offers a unique lodging experience with rooms featuring artistic decor. Guests can enjoy meals at the on-site restaurant and live music events.

2. Study Butte

Overview:
Located just a few miles from Terlingua, Study Butte is a small community that serves as another convenient base for exploring Big Bend. It offers a mix of accommodations and dining options.

Accommodations:

Big Bend Resort and Adventures

Address: 2101 TX-118, Study Butte, TX 79852

Contact: (432) 371-3382

Website: https://www.bigbendresort.com

Price: $95 to $250 per night (varies by accommodation type)

Description: This resort offers a variety of options, including motel rooms, cabins, and RV sites. Amenities include a restaurant and an outdoor pool, making it a great place to relax after a day of exploring.

Lajitas Golf Resort

Address: 100 Main St, Lajitas, TX 79852

Contact: (877) 525-4827

Website: https://www.lajitasgolfresort.com

Price: $150 to $350 per night (varies by season and room type)

Description: Located about 30 minutes from the park, this resort offers luxurious accommodations and amenities, including a golf course, spa, and multiple dining options.

3. Alpine

Overview:

Alpine is a larger town located about 30 miles (48 kilometers) from the park entrance. It offers more services, including shopping, dining, and a variety of accommodations.

Accommodations:

Comfort Inn & Suites

    Address: 2601 W Highway 90, Alpine, TX 79830

    Contact: (432) 837-1000

    Price: $120 to $180 per night (varies by season)

    Description: This hotel offers comfortable rooms with modern amenities, including a fitness center, free breakfast, and Wi-Fi. It's a good choice for families and travelers looking for convenience.

The Holland Hotel

    Address: 800 W Holland Ave, Alpine, TX 79830

Contact: (432) 837-2111

Website: https://www.thehollandhotel.com

Price: $110 to $200 per night (varies by room type)

Description: A historic hotel with a charming atmosphere, the Holland Hotel offers comfortable accommodations and is conveniently located near downtown Alpine. The hotel features a restaurant and bar on-site.

4. Marathon

Overview:

Marathon is a small town located about 30 miles (48 kilometers) from the park entrance. It's known for its scenic beauty and laid-back atmosphere, making it a nice place to relax after a day of hiking.

Accommodations:

Gage Hotel

Address: 102 N. Gage St, Marathon, TX 79842

Contact: (432) 386-4205

Website: https://www.gagehotel.com

Price: $150 to $300 per night (varies by room type)

Description: This historic hotel features beautifully decorated rooms and offers a restaurant, bar, and outdoor pool. It's a perfect spot to unwind and enjoy the peaceful surroundings.

Marathon Motel

Address: 1021 N. Hwy 90, Marathon, TX 79842

Contact: (432) 386-4444

Price: $85 to $120 per night (varies by season)

Description: A budget-friendly option, the Marathon Motel offers clean and comfortable rooms. It's conveniently located near restaurants and shops in town.

Knowing about nearby towns and accommodations is vital for planning your trip to Big Bend National Park. Whether you prefer the convenience of hotels or the charm of local inns, there are plenty of options to suit your budget and preferences. Make sure to book your accommodations in advance, especially during peak seasons, to ensure a comfortable stay while you explore the breathtaking landscapes and outdoor adventures that Big Bend has to offer.

4. Park Overview

4.1 Geography and Climate

Big Bend National Park is a vast and beautiful area located in West Texas, near the border with Mexico. The park is known for its stunning landscapes, diverse ecosystems, and unique geology. Understanding the geography and climate of Big Bend is essential for planning your visit and making the most of your experience.

Geography

1. Size and Location:
Big Bend National Park covers approximately 801,000 acres (about 1,200 square miles), making it one of the largest national parks in the United States. It is located in Brewster County, about 100 miles (160 kilometers) southeast of El Paso and 80 miles (129 kilometers) from the nearest town, Alpine.

2. Terrain:
The park's geography is diverse and features a variety of landscapes, including:

Mountains:
The Chisos Mountains are the most prominent feature in the park, rising over 7,800 feet (2,400 meters) at their highest point, Emory Peak. These mountains are surrounded by lush vegetation, making them a stark contrast to the surrounding desert.

Deserts:
The lower elevations of the park are characterized by arid desert landscapes. The

Chihuahuan Desert, which covers much of West Texas, is home to a unique array of plant and animal life, including cacti, yucca, and various desert-dwelling animals.

River:
The Rio Grande River forms the southern boundary of the park and serves as the natural border between the United States and Mexico. The river creates stunning canyons and offers opportunities for river-based activities such as canoeing and kayaking.

Canyons:
The park is home to dramatic canyons, including the famous Santa Elena Canyon, which features towering cliffs and beautiful views of the river below. The canyons provide excellent hiking opportunities and a chance to explore the park's unique geological formations.

3. Biodiversity:
Big Bend National Park is a biodiversity hotspot, with over 1,200 species of plants and nearly 450 species of birds, mammals, reptiles, and amphibians. The park's varied ecosystems, from the mountains to the desert and the river, support a wide range of wildlife, making it a paradise for nature enthusiasts and birdwatchers.

Climate

1. General Climate:
The climate in Big Bend National Park is classified as arid, with hot summers and mild winters. The park experiences significant temperature variations, so visitors should be prepared for both heat and cooler conditions, especially in the mountains.

2. Seasons:

Summer (June to August):
Summer temperatures can soar, often exceeding 100°F (38°C) in the lower elevations during the day. However, nights can cool down, especially in the mountains. Visitors should plan for early morning hikes to avoid the heat and carry plenty of water to stay hydrated.

Fall (September to November):
Fall is a great time to visit Big Bend, as temperatures become more comfortable. Daytime temperatures range from the mid-70s to mid-80s°F (24-29°C), while nights can be cooler. Fall foliage adds to the park's beauty, especially in the higher elevations.

Winter (December to February):
Winters are mild in the park, but temperatures can drop significantly at night, especially in the mountains. Daytime highs can range from the upper 50s to mid-60s°F (14-18°C), while nighttime lows may drop below freezing. Snow is rare but can occur in the higher elevations.

Spring (March to May):
Spring is another excellent time to visit, with temperatures gradually warming. Daytime highs typically range from the 70s to 90s°F (21-37°C). Wildflowers bloom throughout the park, making for a colorful display against the desert landscape.

3. Rainfall:
Big Bend receives very little rainfall, averaging around 12-20 inches (30-51 cm) per year, with most precipitation occurring in late summer and early fall. Thunderstorms can develop quickly, especially in the summer months, so visitors should be aware of weather conditions while hiking or camping.

The geography and climate of Big Bend National Park contribute to its unique beauty and diverse ecosystems. From the rugged mountains to the arid desert and the winding Rio Grande, the park offers visitors a chance to experience nature in its many forms. Understanding these elements will help you prepare for your trip, ensuring you can enjoy all that Big Bend has to offer while staying safe and comfortable in this stunning natural environment.

4.2 Flora and Fauna

Big Bend National Park is a remarkable place known for its rich diversity of plants and animals. The park's unique geography and climate create various habitats that support a wide range of flora and fauna. Here's a closer look at what you can expect to see when you visit.

Flora (Plants)

1. Types of Vegetation:
Big Bend National Park is home to over 1,200 species of plants, which thrive in its different environments, from desert to mountains. Here are some of the main types of vegetation you will find:

Desert Plants:
The Chihuahuan Desert, which covers much of the park, is filled with drought-resistant plants. Common species include:

Cacti: Various types of cacti, such as the iconic prickly pear and the tall organ pipe cactus, dot the landscape. Cacti have thick, fleshy stems that store water, helping them survive in dry conditions.

Yucca: This spiky plant is known for its tall flower stalks that bloom with white flowers in the spring. The leaves are long and sharp, creating a striking appearance.

Agave: The agave plant is known for its rosette shape and spiky leaves. It can take many years to flower, producing a tall stalk of flowers before the plant dies, a phenomenon known as monocarpic flowering.

Grasslands:
In the lower elevations, you will find open grasslands filled with native grasses and wildflowers. These areas provide important habitats for many animals.

Riparian Zones:
Areas along the Rio Grande and its tributaries support lush vegetation, including willows, cottonwoods, and other moisture-loving plants. These zones are critical for wildlife, providing food and shelter.

Mountain Forests:
In the higher elevations of the Chisos Mountains, the flora changes dramatically. Here, you'll find:

Pines: The park is home to several species of pine trees, such as the ponderosa pine, which thrive in the cooler, moist mountain environment.

Oak Trees: Different types of oak trees, like the Mexican oak, can be found in the Chisos Mountains, providing shade and habitat for various animals.

2. Seasonal Changes:
Flora in Big Bend changes with the seasons. Spring brings vibrant wildflower blooms, including desert marigolds and bluebonnets. In summer, many plants are in full leaf and may bloom, while autumn can showcase beautiful fall colors, especially in the higher elevations. Winter is quieter, with many plants going dormant, but some remain green and provide food for wildlife.

Fauna (Animals)

1. Mammals:

Big Bend is home to a wide variety of mammals, including both large and small species. Some notable mammals you might see include:

BigHorn Sheep: These impressive animals can often be spotted on the rocky slopes of the Chisos Mountains. They have curved horns and are well adapted to climbing steep terrain.

Coyotes: Common in the park, coyotes are highly adaptable and can be found in various habitats. They are often heard howling at night.

Javelinas: Also known as collared peccaries, these pig-like animals roam in groups and are usually active during dawn and dusk.

Mountain Lions: These elusive cats are present in the park but are rarely seen. They prefer remote areas and are mostly active at night.

2. Birds:

Big Bend is a birdwatcher's paradise, with nearly 450 species of birds recorded in the park. Some highlights include:

Golden Eagles: These majestic birds of prey can be seen soaring above the mountains, especially during the winter months.

Mexican Jay: Common in the Chisos Mountains, these birds are social and often seen in groups.

Lesser Goldfinch: This small, colorful bird is often found in the lower elevations, flitting about in search of seeds.

Western Bluebirds: These vibrant blue birds are frequently spotted in the park and are a favorite among birdwatchers.

3. Reptiles and Amphibians:

Big Bend has a diverse range of reptiles, thanks to its warm climate. Some notable species include:

Western Diamondback Rattlesnake: This common snake is recognizable by its distinctive rattling sound. It plays an important role in the park's ecosystem.

Desert Tortoise: A slow-moving creature that spends much of its life in burrows to escape the heat. It's a protected species in many areas of its range.

Frogs and Toads: Several species of frogs and toads inhabit the park, typically found near water sources. Their calls can be heard in the evenings, especially during the warmer months.

4. Insects and Other Wildlife:

Insects play a crucial role in the park's ecosystem. You can find various butterflies, bees, and beetles, which are essential for pollination. Additionally, the park is home to numerous other species, including:

Mule Deer: Often seen grazing in the evenings, mule deer are a common sight in the park. They have large ears and a distinctive tail that flashes white.

Bats: Big Bend is home to several bat species, which are essential for insect control. They are most active at night and can often be seen flying around, especially near water sources.

The flora and fauna of Big Bend National Park are a vital part of what makes the park so special. The diverse ecosystems support a rich variety of plant and animal life, each adapted to thrive in this unique environment. Whether you're hiking through the desert, exploring the mountains, or wandering along the river, you'll encounter the incredible beauty of nature and the vibrant life that calls Big Bend home. Understanding this diversity will enhance your appreciation of the park and make your visit even more memorable.

4.3 Cultural and Historical Significance

Big Bend National Park is not just a natural wonder; it is also rich in cultural and historical significance. The park has been home to various peoples and cultures for thousands of years, each leaving its mark on the land. Understanding this history enhances the experience of visiting the park and helps us appreciate its importance beyond its stunning landscapes.

1. Indigenous Peoples

1.1 Native American Tribes:
Long before Europeans arrived, the area now known as Big Bend was inhabited by various Native American tribes. These groups included the Chisos, who are believed to have lived in the region for over 10,000 years. They thrived on the land, relying on its resources for food, shelter, and materials.

Cultural Practices:
The Chisos and other tribes had deep spiritual connections to the land. They engaged in hunting, gathering, and farming, using their knowledge of the environment to survive. Rock art, including petroglyphs, can still be found in the park, telling the stories of these early inhabitants.

1.2 The Importance of the Rio Grande:
The Rio Grande River, which forms the southern boundary of the park, was crucial for the indigenous people. It provided water, food, and a means of transportation. The river also held spiritual significance, as it represented life and sustenance.

2. European Exploration and Settlement

2.1 Spanish Exploration:
In the 16th century, Spanish explorers began to venture into the area. They were drawn by the land's potential for settlement and trade. The Spanish influence is still evident today in place names and cultural practices.

Mission and Ranching:
By the 18th century, Spanish missionaries established missions to convert Native Americans to Christianity. The ranching culture also developed during this period, leading to the establishment of ranches in the region.

2.2 The Mexican-American War:
In the mid-19th century, the area became embroiled in political conflict. The Mexican-American War (1846-1848) changed the boundaries of the region, with Texas becoming a part of the United States. This historical event significantly impacted the people living in and around Big Bend, shaping the cultural landscape of the area.

3. The Birth of Big Bend National Park

3.1 Establishment of the Park:
Big Bend was designated as a national park in 1944, but the efforts to preserve the area began much earlier. Local citizens and conservationists recognized the park's unique landscapes and ecosystems and fought for its protection.

Significant Figures:
One of the key figures in the park's establishment was J. Frank Dobie, a writer and folklorist

who advocated for the region's preservation. His writings helped raise awareness of Big Bend's natural beauty and cultural significance.

3.2 Cultural Heritage:

Since its establishment, Big Bend National Park has become a place where visitors can learn about the area's cultural heritage. The park offers educational programs, guided tours, and cultural demonstrations that highlight the history and traditions of the indigenous peoples and early settlers.

4. Historic Structures and Sites

4.1 Ranching History:

Within the park, you can find remnants of the ranching history that shaped the region. For example, the ruins of the historic Sam Nail Ranch provide insight into early settler life. The ranch was established in the early 1900s and was home to a family that worked the land.

Visitor Center Exhibits:

The park's visitor centers also feature exhibits that showcase the history of ranching, mining, and the indigenous peoples of the area. These resources help visitors understand the diverse cultural narratives that have unfolded in Big Bend.

4.2 The Ghost Town of Terlingua:

Located just outside the park, Terlingua was once a bustling mercury mining town. Today, it is a ghost town that attracts visitors interested in its history. The remnants of old buildings and the unique desert landscape create a glimpse into the past.

5. Modern Cultural Significance

5.1 Art and Inspiration:

Big Bend continues to inspire artists, writers, and photographers. The stunning landscapes and diverse wildlife serve as a backdrop for creativity. Many visitors come to capture the park's beauty and connect with nature.

5.2 Outdoor Recreation and Community:

Today, Big Bend National Park is a popular destination for outdoor recreation, including hiking, camping, and stargazing. The park's cultural significance extends to modern-day activities, where visitors engage with the land in ways that honor its history.

5.3 Cultural Events:

Throughout the year, the park hosts various cultural events and programs that celebrate the region's history. These events often include traditional music, storytelling, and art exhibitions, providing a platform for local artists and community members to share their heritage.

Big Bend National Park is a place where nature and culture intertwine. Its rich history, from ancient indigenous peoples to early settlers and modern conservation efforts, tells a story of resilience and connection to the land. By understanding the cultural and historical significance of Big Bend, visitors can deepen their appreciation for this remarkable park, making their experience not just a visit to a national park but a journey through time.

5. Things to Do

5.1 Hiking Trails

Big Bend National Park is a hiker's paradise, offering a wide range of trails that cater to different skill levels and preferences. Whether you're a seasoned hiker or just looking for a leisurely walk, there's something for everyone. Here's an overview of the popular trails and some hidden gems that are worth exploring.

5.1.1 Popular Trails: Overview and Difficulty Levels

1. Lost Mine Trail

Distance: 4.8 miles round trip

Difficulty Level: Moderate

Overview:
The Lost Mine Trail is one of the most popular hikes in the park. It starts at the pine tree-lined Chisos Basin and gradually climbs to a ridge that offers breathtaking views of the surrounding mountains and valleys. Along the way, hikers will encounter diverse plant life and possibly spot some wildlife. The final stretch to the viewpoint is steep, but the panoramic views at the top make the effort worthwhile.

2. Window Trail

Distance: 5.6 miles round trip

Difficulty Level: Moderate

Overview:
The Window Trail is another must-do hike that takes you to a dramatic overlook where the Chisos Mountains appear to "drop off" into the desert below. The trail winds through oak and pine forests, with stunning rock formations and a variety of wildflowers along the way. The best time to hike this trail is during the early morning or late afternoon, as the lighting enhances the beauty of the view.

3. Emory Peak Trail

Distance: 10.5 miles round trip

Difficulty Level: Strenuous

Overview:
For those looking for a challenge, the Emory Peak Trail leads to the highest point in the park, standing at 7,832 feet. The hike involves a steep ascent, but the views from the summit are absolutely breathtaking, offering a 360-degree panorama of Big Bend and beyond. Hikers should be prepared for changing weather conditions, especially at higher elevations.

4. Chisos Basin Loop Trail

Distance: 4.8 miles round trip

Difficulty Level: Easy to Moderate

Overview:
This trail offers a great way to explore the Chisos Basin area without committing to a longer hike. It meanders through the basin, showcasing a variety of landscapes, including forested areas and open fields. The trail is well-maintained and suitable for families, making it a great option for a leisurely hike.

5.1.2 Hidden Gems: Lesser-Known Trails

1. Lost Mine Trail (for Early Birds)

Distance: 4.8 miles round trip

Difficulty Level: Moderate

Overview:
While this trail is known, many hikers overlook it in favor of more famous routes. By starting early in the morning, you can enjoy a quieter experience with fewer crowds. The sunrise views from the trail are spectacular, as the sun casts beautiful colors over the mountains.

2. Pine Canyon Trail

Distance: 4 miles round trip

Difficulty Level: Moderate

Overview:
This lesser-known trail offers a peaceful hike through a canyon filled with towering pines and impressive rock formations. The trail descends into the canyon, where you can enjoy the cool shade of the trees. Wildlife, such as deer and birds, can often be spotted along this route. It's a great option for those looking to escape the busier trails.

3. The Gcha'ah Trail (formerly known as the Gcha'ah Loop)

Distance: 3.5 miles round trip

Difficulty Level: Easy to Moderate

Overview:

This trail is a hidden gem that offers a unique perspective of the park's landscapes. It takes you through diverse habitats, including desert scrub and riparian zones along the river. It's less traveled than other trails, allowing for a quieter experience where you can appreciate the natural beauty and listen to the sounds of nature.

4. Black Gap Road Trail

Distance: 6 miles round trip

Difficulty Level: Strenuous

Overview:

For the adventurous hiker, the Black Gap Road Trail leads to a remote area of the park that few visitors explore. This trail offers a rugged experience with stunning views of the surrounding mountains and canyons. Hikers should be well-prepared, as the terrain can be challenging, and it's essential to bring plenty of water.

Hiking in Big Bend National Park is a fantastic way to experience its natural beauty, with a variety of trails that cater to all skill levels. From popular paths that showcase the park's stunning vistas to hidden gems that offer solitude and tranquility, there is something for everyone. Make sure to choose a trail that matches your abilities, and don't forget to pack plenty of water and snacks for your adventure. Whether you're tackling a challenging summit or enjoying a leisurely stroll, the breathtaking landscapes of Big Bend await you!

5.2 Wildlife Watching

Big Bend National Park is not only known for its stunning landscapes but also for its incredible wildlife. The park is home to a diverse array of animals, making it a fantastic destination for wildlife watching. Whether you're a seasoned birdwatcher or just love seeing animals in their natural habitat, Big Bend offers plenty of opportunities to connect with nature.

5.2.1 Birding Opportunities

1. Diverse Bird Species

Big Bend is a paradise for bird enthusiasts, with nearly 450 species of birds recorded in the park. The variety of habitats—from deserts and mountains to rivers and forests—supports a wide range of avian life. Here are some key highlights for birdwatching:

Migratory Birds:

The park is a stopover for many migratory birds, especially during spring and fall. You can spot colorful warblers, flycatchers, and hummingbirds as they travel between their wintering and breeding grounds.

Resident Birds:

Many birds call Big Bend home year-round. Look for species like:

Golden Eagles: Often seen soaring high in the sky, especially during winter.

Mexican Jays: These social birds can be spotted in the Chisos Mountains, often seen in groups.

Greater Roadrunner: Famous for its speed, this bird can be spotted darting across the desert floor.

2. Best Locations for Bird Watching

Certain areas in the park are particularly good for birdwatching:

Rio Grande Village:

This area is known for its diverse bird population, especially near the river. Look for herons, ducks, and other waterfowl. The birding is especially good during early morning and late afternoon.

Chisos Basin:

The higher elevation attracts different species, including hawks and mountain birds. The trails around the basin are excellent for spotting various birds throughout the year.

Santa Elena Canyon:

The towering cliffs and the river create a unique habitat for birds. Keep an eye out for swallows and other cliff-nesting species.

3. Tips for Bird Watching

To make the most of your birding experience, consider these tips:

Bring Binoculars:

A good pair of binoculars will help you get a closer look at distant birds without disturbing them.

Early Mornings:

The best time for birdwatching is often early in the morning when birds are most active.

Patience is Key:

Wildlife watching requires patience. Spend time quietly observing your surroundings, and you'll be surprised at what you can see.

5.2.2 Mammal and Reptile Sightings

1. Mammal Species
Big Bend is home to a variety of mammals, from large to small. Here are some of the most commonly spotted animals:

Deer:
Mule deer are frequently seen, especially in the mornings and evenings. They often graze in the open meadows and along the trails.

Coyotes:
Coyotes are active throughout the park and are often heard howling at night. They are most visible during the early morning or late evening when they are out hunting.

Javelinas:
These pig-like animals can be seen wandering in groups. They are often active during dawn and dusk, making early morning hikes a good time to spot them.

Mountain Lions:
Though elusive and rarely seen, mountain lions do inhabit the park. If you're lucky, you might spot one in the early morning or late evening, but keep your distance if you do.

2. Reptile Sightings
The warm climate of Big Bend supports a variety of reptiles. Here are some you might encounter:

Rattlesnakes:
The Western Diamondback Rattlesnake is common in the park. While they are generally not aggressive, it's essential to watch where you step and to be cautious while hiking.

Lizards:
Various species of lizards, such as the Collared Lizard, can be seen basking on rocks or darting across the trails. They are active during the warmer months.

Desert Tortoises:
While less common, you may spot a desert tortoise in more remote areas of the park. They spend much of their time hidden but can sometimes be seen near water sources.

3. Best Times for Mammal and Reptile Watching
To maximize your chances of spotting mammals and reptiles, consider the following:

Early Mornings and Late Afternoons:

Many animals are more active during the cooler parts of the day. Early mornings and late afternoons are the best times to see wildlife.

Quiet Observation:

Move slowly and quietly to avoid startling animals. Sometimes, just sitting quietly and waiting can yield incredible wildlife sightings.

Look for Tracks and Signs:

If you're not able to spot animals directly, look for tracks, droppings, or other signs of wildlife activity. This can add an exciting dimension to your experience.

Wildlife watching in Big Bend National Park is an unforgettable experience. With its diverse bird species and abundant mammals and reptiles, the park offers something for every nature lover. Whether you're hiking a trail, sitting quietly by the river, or exploring the canyons, keep your eyes peeled for the incredible wildlife that calls this beautiful park home. Remember to respect the animals and observe from a distance, allowing them to thrive in their natural habitat while you enjoy the wonders of nature.

5.3 Camping and Lodging

Big Bend National Park is an excellent destination for those who love to immerse themselves in nature, and camping is one of the best ways to experience the park's beauty. Whether you prefer traditional campgrounds or backcountry camping, Big Bend has options for everyone. Additionally, there are lodges and cabins for those who prefer a more comfortable stay. Here's a comprehensive look at your camping and lodging options in the park.

5.3.1 Campgrounds: Reservations and Amenities

Big Bend National Park offers several campgrounds, each with its unique charm and amenities. Here's an overview of the main campgrounds:

1. Chisos Basin Campground

Overview:
Located at an elevation of 5,400 feet, this campground is surrounded by the stunning Chisos Mountains. It is a popular spot, especially in spring and fall, offering easy access to several hiking trails.

Reservations:

Reservations are recommended and can be made through the National Park Service website. This campground fills up quickly, especially during peak seasons.

Amenities:

> **Number of Sites:** 60

> **Facilities:** Restrooms, picnic tables, and fire rings are available.

> **Water:** Drinking water is provided, but campers should bring their own water for cooking and cleaning.

2. Rio Grande Village Campground

Overview:

Situated along the Rio Grande, this campground offers a unique desert setting. It's an excellent choice for families and those wanting to explore the nearby river and wildlife.

Reservations:

Reservations are recommended but not required during the off-peak season. It's best to check the availability before your visit.

Amenities:

> **Number of Sites:** 25

> **Facilities:** Restrooms, picnic tables, and fire rings are provided.

> **Water:** Drinking water is available, and there are nearby restrooms.

3. Cottonwood Campground

Overview:

This smaller, quieter campground is located near the Cottonwood trees along the Rio Grande. It's ideal for those looking for a more peaceful camping experience.

Reservations:

Reservations are recommended, especially in peak seasons.

Amenities:

> **Number of Sites:** 24

Facilities: Picnic tables, fire rings, and restrooms are available.

Water: Drinking water is accessible, but campers should bring their own water for cooking.

5.3.2 Backcountry Camping Guidelines

For those who crave adventure and solitude, backcountry camping is an excellent option. Here are some important guidelines to follow:

1. Permit Requirements

Before setting out, you must obtain a backcountry camping permit. This can be done at the park's visitor centers or online. Permits are free but required to ensure safety and protect the park's resources.

2. Designated Campsites

While backcountry camping allows you to choose your own spot, it's important to camp at least 1 mile away from established trails and roads. This helps minimize your impact on the environment.

3. Leave No Trace Principles

Follow the Leave No Trace principles to preserve the park's beauty. This includes packing out all trash, minimizing campfire impact, and respecting wildlife.

4. Safety Considerations

Be aware of the weather, as conditions can change rapidly in the park. Bring plenty of water, a reliable map or GPS device, and a first-aid kit. Always let someone know your plans before heading out.

5. Best Practices

Camp in groups of 10 or fewer to reduce impact. Avoid camping in areas that show signs of heavy use. Use established fire rings when available, or consider a camp stove for cooking to reduce fire impact.

5.3.3 Lodges and Cabins

If you prefer more comfort while enjoying the beauty of Big Bend, there are several lodges and cabins nearby. Here's a look at some of your options:

1. Chisos Mountains Lodge

Overview:
This lodge is located in the heart of the Chisos Basin and offers stunning views of the surrounding mountains. It's an excellent base for exploring the park.

Accommodation Types:
The lodge features hotel-style rooms and a restaurant with a menu focusing on local ingredients.

Price Range:
Prices typically range from $140 to $250 per night, depending on the season and type of room. Reservations are highly recommended, especially during peak seasons.

2. Rio Grande Village RV Park

Overview:
This RV park offers a more rustic experience with modern amenities. It's conveniently located near the river, making it a great spot for fishing and kayaking.

Accommodation Types:
The park has RV sites with full hookups and tent sites. Basic amenities include restrooms, showers, and a camp store.

Price Range:
RV sites start around $25 per night, while tent sites are about $15 per night.

3. Terlingua Ghost Town Lodging

Overview:
Just outside the park, Terlingua offers various lodging options, including cabins, motels, and unique accommodations like a converted school bus. This area has a charming ghost town atmosphere, making it an interesting place to stay.

Accommodation Types:
Options range from basic motels to fully equipped cabins with kitchen facilities.

Price Range:
Prices vary widely, from $80 for basic rooms to $200 for more upscale cabins. It's advisable to book in advance, especially during busy travel seasons.

Whether you choose to camp under the stars, explore the backcountry, or stay in a cozy lodge, Big Bend National Park has accommodations to suit every preference. Camping allows for a deeper connection with the park's stunning landscapes, while lodges provide comfort and convenience. No matter where you stay, the beauty of Big Bend will enhance your experience and create lasting memories. Remember to plan ahead, especially during peak seasons, to ensure you have the best options available for your visit.

5.4 Scenic Drives

Big Bend National Park is not only about hiking and wildlife; it also offers some of the most breathtaking scenic drives in Texas. These drives provide a wonderful way to experience the park's stunning landscapes, diverse ecosystems, and unique geological formations—all from the comfort of your vehicle. Here's a look at two of the most popular scenic drives in the park: the Ross Maxwell Scenic Drive and Old Maverick Road.

5.4.1 Ross Maxwell Scenic Drive

Overview
The Ross Maxwell Scenic Drive is one of the highlights of Big Bend National Park, stretching approximately 30 miles from the Panther Junction Visitor Center to the Santa Elena Canyon. This drive showcases some of the most spectacular landscapes in the park, offering breathtaking views of the Chisos Mountains, vast desert expanses, and stunning rock formations.

Key Stops Along the Drive

Sotol Vista:
Just a few miles into the drive, stop at the Sotol Vista overlook for a panoramic view of the Chihuahuan Desert and the distant Sierra del Carmen mountains. It's a great spot for photography, especially at sunrise or sunset when the colors are vibrant.

Sam Nail Ranch:
This historic site offers a glimpse into the past, where you can see the remnants of an early ranching operation. There are picnic tables available for a lunch stop, and you can take a short hike to the nearby springs.

Burro Mesa Pouroff:
This area features a short, easy hike to a beautiful waterfall. While the water may not flow year-round, the surrounding scenery is beautiful and worth exploring. The hike is less than a mile round trip and offers a close-up view of the unique geology of the area.

Santa Elena Canyon:

The drive ends at the entrance to Santa Elena Canyon, a must-see destination. Here, you can walk along the river and gaze up at the towering cliffs that rise 1,500 feet above the Rio Grande. The views here are stunning, especially during the late afternoon when the sun casts beautiful shadows on the canyon walls.

Driving Tips

Time to Allow:

Plan for at least two to three hours to drive the full route, including time for stops and exploration. If you want to take longer hikes or enjoy the overlooks, consider setting aside a whole day.

Road Conditions:

The road is well-maintained, but be aware of possible wildlife crossings, especially during dawn and dusk. Always drive cautiously and be prepared for changing weather conditions.

5.4.2 Old Maverick Road

Overview

Old Maverick Road offers a different kind of scenic drive, allowing you to experience the rugged beauty of Big Bend at a slower pace. This unpaved road runs approximately 12 miles from the entrance of the park to the Rio Grande Village area, taking you through desert landscapes, rugged mountains, and unique rock formations.

Key Features Along the Drive

Cerro Castellan:

This distinctive cone-shaped mountain is a landmark in the park and offers stunning views. Pull over at the viewpoint for a closer look and some great photo opportunities.

Tuff Canyon:

Along the route, you'll come across Tuff Canyon, known for its colorful rock layers and steep walls. There are short trails that lead into the canyon for those who want to explore further.

Old West Feel:

The road has a more rustic, Wild West atmosphere compared to the paved drives. You'll feel a sense of solitude as you drive through this remote part of the park. Keep an eye out for local wildlife, including deer, coyotes, and various bird species.

Driving Tips

Vehicle Requirements:
Since Old Maverick Road is unpaved, a high-clearance vehicle is recommended. However, many sedans can navigate the road, especially if conditions are dry. Just be cautious and drive slowly to avoid bumps.

Best Time to Visit:
The best time to drive Old Maverick Road is during the cooler months, from late fall to early spring. Summer temperatures can be intense, making the drive less enjoyable.

Safety Precautions:
Always carry plenty of water, especially if you plan to stop and explore the areas along the way. There are limited services in the park, so be prepared for a remote experience.

Both the Ross Maxwell Scenic Drive and Old Maverick Road offer unique and unforgettable ways to experience the breathtaking beauty of Big Bend National Park. Whether you prefer the well-maintained routes and spectacular views of the Ross Maxwell Drive or the rugged charm of Old Maverick Road, you'll find plenty of opportunities for stunning scenery and adventure. Don't forget your camera, pack some snacks, and take your time to soak in the awe-inspiring landscapes that make Big Bend a must-visit destination!

5.5 Photography Spots

Big Bend National Park is a photographer's paradise, offering stunning landscapes, vibrant wildlife, and mesmerizing night skies. Whether you are a professional photographer or a casual snapper, you'll find countless opportunities to capture the beauty of this unique park. Here's a look at some of the best photography spots and tips for getting the most out of your experience.

5.5.1 Iconic Landscapes and Sunsets

Big Bend is known for its breathtaking landscapes that change dramatically with the time of day. Here are some must-visit spots for capturing iconic views:

1. Santa Elena Canyon

Overview:
This canyon features towering cliffs that rise up to 1,500 feet above the Rio Grande. The contrasting colors of the rock face and the blue river create a dramatic scene.

Best Time to Visit:
Late afternoon and sunset are the best times to photograph Santa Elena Canyon. The sunlight casts warm hues on the canyon walls, enhancing their beauty.

2. Chisos Basin

Overview:
The Chisos Mountains provide a stunning backdrop for photography. The combination of rugged peaks and vibrant wildflowers in the spring creates a picturesque setting.

Best Time to Visit:
Early morning or late afternoon offers the best light for capturing the mountains, as the sun rises or sets behind them, casting beautiful shadows.

3. Sotol Vista

Overview:
This overlook provides sweeping views of the desert below and the distant Sierra del Carmen mountains. The vastness of the landscape makes for stunning wide-angle shots.

Best Time to Visit:
Sunset is particularly magical here, as the sun dips below the horizon, creating a colorful sky that complements the desert landscape.

4. Burro Mesa Pouroff

Overview:
This area is known for its unique geological features, including dramatic cliffs and a seasonal waterfall. The contrasting textures and colors are ideal for photography.

Best Time to Visit:
Early morning light highlights the rock formations beautifully, making it a great time to capture detailed shots.

5. The Window

Overview:
A popular hiking destination in the Chisos Basin, the Window is a natural rock formation that frames the desert view below. The hike itself offers numerous photo opportunities.

Best Time to Visit:
Late afternoon and sunset are the best times, as the light filtering through the Window creates an ethereal glow.

5.5.2 Astrophotography Tips

Big Bend National Park is renowned for its dark skies, making it one of the best places in the United States for astrophotography. Here are some tips to help you capture the beauty of the night sky:

1. Find a Dark Spot

Overview:
The best astrophotography results come from locations far from city lights. Big Bend's remote areas are perfect for stargazing. Popular spots include the Chisos Basin, Cottonwood Campground, and the Rio Grande Village.

2. Check the Moon Phase

Overview:
The brightness of the moon can wash out faint stars and celestial objects. Plan your trip during a new moon or when the moon is below the horizon for the darkest skies.

3. Use the Right Equipment

Camera:
A DSLR or mirrorless camera with manual settings is ideal for astrophotography. A camera with good low-light performance will yield better results.

Lenses:
A wide-angle lens (between 14mm to 24mm) with a large aperture (f/2.8 or wider) will help capture more of the sky and allow more light in.

Tripod:
A sturdy tripod is essential for long exposures, which are necessary for capturing stars without blurriness.

4. Settings to Use

ISO:
Start with an ISO of 1600 to 3200. Higher ISO values will capture more light but can introduce noise.

Aperture:
Set your lens to its widest aperture (f/2.8 or lower) to allow as much light in as possible.

Shutter Speed:
For star trails, use a longer exposure (up to 30 seconds). If you want to capture stars as points, use the 500 rule: divide 500 by your lens focal length to find the maximum exposure time in seconds.

5. Plan Ahead

Apps:
Use apps like SkySafari or Star Walk to help you locate constellations, planets, and other celestial objects. These tools can also help you plan your shots based on the time and location of the Milky Way.

Weather:
Check the weather forecast to ensure clear skies for your astrophotography session. Clouds can obstruct your view of the stars.

With its stunning landscapes and incredibly dark skies, Big Bend National Park offers photographers endless opportunities for capturing nature's beauty. Whether you're interested in stunning sunset landscapes or capturing the Milky Way, this park has something for everyone. Plan your visits to these iconic spots and prepare for an unforgettable photography experience in one of the most beautiful places in Texas!

6. Adventure Activities

6.1 River Activities: Canoeing and Kayaking

One of the most exciting ways to experience Big Bend National Park is by exploring its rivers, particularly the Rio Grande. The river offers a range of activities for all skill levels, from leisurely paddles to more challenging excursions. Here's a comprehensive guide to canoeing and kayaking in Big Bend, including what to expect, where to go, and tips for a safe and enjoyable experience.

Overview of the Rio Grande

Rio Grande

The Rio Grande runs along the border between the United States and Mexico, providing stunning views of the surrounding desert and mountains. The river features varying conditions, from calm stretches perfect for beginners to more challenging sections ideal for experienced paddlers. The scenery along the river is diverse, with opportunities to see wildlife, dramatic rock formations, and the iconic canyons that define this part of Texas.

Types of River Activities

1. Canoeing

Canoeing is a great option for families and those looking for a relaxed experience on the water. Canoes provide stability and ample space for gear, making them suitable for longer trips.

Guided Tours:

For those unfamiliar with the river, joining a guided canoe tour is an excellent way to explore safely. Local outfitters offer guided excursions that include equipment rental, safety instruction, and experienced guides who know the best spots along the river.

Self-Guided Trips:

If you're experienced and want to paddle at your own pace, you can rent a canoe and set off on a self-guided adventure. Popular launch points include the Rio Grande Village and the put-in location at the Santa Elena Canyon.

2. Kayaking

Kayaking is ideal for those seeking a more adventurous experience. Kayaks are generally faster and more maneuverable than canoes, allowing for a thrilling ride down the river.

Recreational Kayaks:

These are perfect for calm waters and beginners. They are wider and more stable, making them suitable for leisurely paddling and sightseeing.

Sit-on-top Kayaks:

These are great for warmer days, allowing for easy entry and exit from the kayak. They provide good stability and are perfect for short trips on the river.

Whitewater Kayaking:
For experienced paddlers, certain sections of the Rio Grande offer exciting rapids and challenging conditions. The stretch between the Mariscal Canyon and the Santa Elena Canyon is known for its thrilling whitewater.

Best Locations for River Activities

1. Santa Elena Canyon

Overview:
This is one of the most beautiful sections of the Rio Grande, featuring towering cliffs that rise dramatically from the water. Paddling through the canyon offers a unique perspective of the park's stunning geology.

Trip Duration:
The paddle through the canyon can take 2 to 4 hours, depending on your pace and water conditions. Be sure to check for water levels, as they can affect your trip.

2. Rio Grande Village

Overview:
This area offers easy access to the river and is suitable for both canoeing and kayaking. The waters here are typically calm, making it an excellent spot for beginners and families.

Amenities:
Facilities at Rio Grande Village include restrooms and picnic areas, making it a convenient location to start and end your river adventure.

3. Mariscal Canyon

Overview:
Known for its dramatic cliffs and stunning views, Mariscal Canyon offers a more remote paddling experience. This area is recommended for more experienced paddlers, especially those looking for some excitement.

Trip Duration:
The trip through Mariscal Canyon can take a full day, with opportunities to camp along the way for those seeking a multi-day adventure.

Safety Considerations

Check Water Levels:
Before heading out, check the current water conditions and weather forecasts. High water levels can create dangerous conditions, especially in the whitewater areas.

Wear Life Jackets:
Always wear a personal flotation device (PFD) while on the water, regardless of your experience level. It's a simple safety measure that can save lives.

Stay Hydrated and Pack Essentials:
Bring plenty of water, snacks, sunscreen, and a first-aid kit. The desert sun can be intense, so staying hydrated is crucial.

Know Your Limits:
Assess your skill level and choose an activity that matches your experience. If you're a beginner, stick to calmer sections of the river.

Leave No Trace:
Be respectful of the environment by packing out all trash and minimizing your impact on the river and surrounding areas.

Canoeing and kayaking in Big Bend National Park provide unforgettable adventures for outdoor enthusiasts. Whether you're gliding through the tranquil waters of the Rio Grande or navigating thrilling rapids, the river offers unique perspectives of the park's stunning landscapes. With careful planning, safety precautions, and respect for the environment, you can enjoy an exhilarating day on the water in one of America's most beautiful national parks!

6.2 Rock Climbing and Bouldering

Big Bend National Park is not just a haven for hikers and paddlers; it's also an exciting destination for rock climbers and bouldering enthusiasts. The park's dramatic landscapes, towering cliffs, and unique rock formations provide countless opportunities for climbers of all skill levels. Whether you're a seasoned climber or a beginner looking to try something new, here's everything you need to know about rock climbing and bouldering in Big Bend.

Overview of Rock Climbing in Big Bend

The park features a variety of climbing areas, each offering a unique experience. The rock types include limestone, granite, and volcanic tuff, providing diverse climbing opportunities. The most popular climbing locations include the Chisos Mountains and the surrounding desert cliffs, where you'll find routes ranging from beginner-friendly to advanced.

Key Climbing Areas:

Chisos Mountains:

> **Overview:**
> The Chisos Mountains are home to some of the best climbing routes in the park. The terrain offers both trad (traditional) and sport climbing options, with routes suitable for climbers of all levels.
>
> **Popular Routes:**

The South Face of the Chisos: Features routes like the popular "Wilderness" (5.8) and "Monk's Path" (5.9), providing stunning views and challenging climbs.

Emory Peak: This area offers multi-pitch climbing with excellent rock quality.

Maverick Road Area:

Overview:
Located near the entrance of the park, this area features several climbing spots with easy access and a variety of routes.

Popular Routes:

The "Maverick" Climbs: Includes routes ranging from 5.6 to 5.11, suitable for various skill levels.

Big Bend Ranch State Park:

Overview:
Just west of Big Bend National Park, this state park offers additional climbing opportunities with beautiful desert backdrops.

Popular Routes:

The "Pecos River" Climbs: A mix of trad and sport routes with beautiful views of the Pecos River.

Bouldering in Big Bend

Bouldering is another popular activity in the park, especially for those looking for a less technical climbing experience. Bouldering involves climbing shorter rock formations without the use of ropes, typically using crash pads for safety.

Popular Bouldering Areas:

The Chisos Basin:

Overview:
This area features several boulders with problems ranging from easy to advanced. The scenic backdrop of the Chisos Mountains makes it an ideal spot for bouldering.

Popular Problems:

Look for routes along the trails, with varying difficulties to cater to both beginners and experienced climbers.

Cottonwood Campground:

Overview:

This campground offers bouldering opportunities close to amenities. Climbers can easily access problems after a day of hiking or enjoying the river.

Popular Problems:

Various bouldering problems are scattered around the campground, providing a fun and relaxed atmosphere.

Climbing Regulations and Safety

When climbing or bouldering in Big Bend National Park, it's essential to follow regulations and safety guidelines to protect both yourself and the park's natural resources.

1. Climbing Regulations:

Always check for any specific regulations or restrictions before climbing, as certain areas may have seasonal closures to protect nesting birds or other wildlife.

Use established routes and avoid creating new ones to preserve the park's natural environment.

2. Safety Precautions:

Gear:
Always use appropriate climbing gear, including harnesses, helmets, and ropes. For bouldering, a crash pad is essential to protect against falls.

Buddy System:
Climb with a partner whenever possible. Having someone with you can provide safety, support, and encouragement.

Weather Awareness:
Be aware of changing weather conditions, especially in the mountains. Avoid climbing during storms or high winds, and be cautious of sudden temperature drops.

Stay Hydrated:

The desert climate can be harsh, so carry plenty of water, especially during hot months. Dehydration can significantly impact your climbing performance and safety.

Conclusion

Rock climbing and bouldering in Big Bend National Park offer unforgettable experiences for adventure seekers. With its diverse terrain, stunning landscapes, and challenging routes, climbers of all skill levels can find something to enjoy. Whether you prefer the thrill of scaling a cliff face or the fun of bouldering with friends, Big Bend provides an exceptional outdoor playground. Remember to prioritize safety, respect the environment, and embrace the adventure that awaits in this beautiful national park!

6.3 Mountain Biking Trails

Mountain biking in Big Bend National Park offers an exhilarating way to explore the park's diverse landscapes, from rugged mountains to desert valleys. With a variety of trails suited for different skill levels, riders can enjoy breathtaking views and the thrill of cycling through this remote and beautiful environment. Here's everything you need to know about mountain biking in Big Bend.

Overview of Mountain Biking in Big Bend

Big Bend National Park features a network of trails that cater to both novice and experienced mountain bikers. The park's terrain varies from smooth, rolling hills to challenging rocky paths, providing a range of experiences for riders. While the park does not have an extensive network of dedicated mountain biking trails, many of the park's roads and multi-use paths are accessible to cyclists, allowing for a unique exploration of the area.

Popular Mountain Biking Trails

1. Old Maverick Road

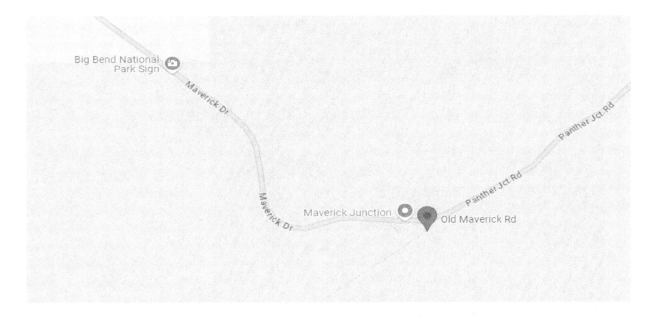

Overview:

This is a 13-mile dirt road that offers stunning views of the desert landscape and is perfect for mountain biking. The road is relatively flat with some rocky sections, making it accessible for most skill levels.

Scenic Highlights:

Along Old Maverick Road, you can enjoy sights like the rugged mountains, open desert plains, and even glimpses of wildlife such as deer and coyotes.

Trail Access:

The road starts near the park entrance, making it an easy and convenient option for bikers.

2. Ross Maxwell Scenic Drive

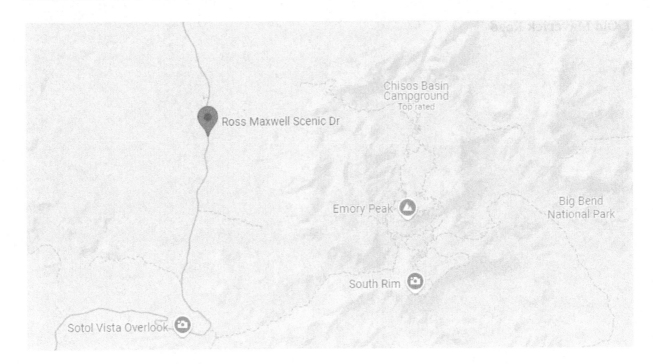

Overview:
While primarily a driving route, portions of Ross Maxwell Scenic Drive can be enjoyed by mountain bikers. This scenic route is known for its breathtaking vistas, including the iconic Santa Elena Canyon.

Scenic Highlights:
Key viewpoints include the Sotol Vista Overlook and the impressive views of the Sierra del Carmen Mountains. Riding here allows you to take in the scenery at a more leisurely pace than driving.

Trail Access:
Bikers can access the drive at various points, with many pull-offs available for stopping and enjoying the scenery.

3. Chisos Basin Loop

Overview:
This loop trail in the Chisos Mountains provides an opportunity for more experienced mountain bikers to tackle some elevation. The trail features a mix of rocky and smooth sections, providing a challenge while rewarding riders with stunning views of the surrounding mountains.

Scenic Highlights:

As you ride, you'll encounter incredible landscapes, including alpine meadows, and diverse flora and fauna.

Trail Access:

The loop begins in the Chisos Basin, where you can also find amenities such as restrooms and picnic areas.

4. Dog Canyon Road

Overview:

This relatively remote area features a rugged road suitable for mountain biking. It offers a true sense of adventure as riders explore the less-traveled parts of the park.

Scenic Highlights:

Riders can experience solitude and witness the unique desert ecosystem while enjoying the stunning views of the surrounding mountains.

Trail Access:

Dog Canyon Road is accessible from the park entrance, and the remoteness of this trail adds to its appeal for those looking for a quieter ride.

Mountain Biking Regulations and Safety

When mountain biking in Big Bend, it's essential to follow park regulations and safety guidelines to protect both yourself and the park's natural resources.

1. Biking Regulations:

Biking is allowed on all paved and unpaved roads within the park but is not permitted on hiking trails. Stick to the designated roads and routes to preserve the natural environment.

Always check for any specific regulations or seasonal closures before heading out.

2. Safety Precautions:

Wear a Helmet:
Always wear a properly fitted helmet while biking to protect yourself in case of falls.

Use the Right Gear:
Ensure your bike is well-maintained and suitable for off-road conditions. A mountain bike with good suspension will help navigate rough terrain more comfortably.

Stay Hydrated:
Carry plenty of water, especially on hot days. Dehydration can impact your performance and safety, so drink regularly.

Be Aware of Weather Conditions:
Weather in the park can change quickly, especially in the mountains. Check forecasts before you head out and be prepared for sudden changes.

Ride with a Buddy:
Whenever possible, bike with a friend. Having a riding partner can enhance safety and make for a more enjoyable experience.

Mountain biking in Big Bend National Park is a fantastic way to explore the park's diverse landscapes while enjoying the thrill of cycling. With a variety of trails suitable for all skill levels, riders can experience the beauty of the park up close. By following safety guidelines and respecting park regulations, you can enjoy a memorable biking adventure in one of Texas's most stunning natural settings. Whether you're cruising along Old Maverick Road or tackling the trails in the Chisos Basin, your time spent mountain biking in Big Bend will surely be an adventure to remember!

6.4 Stargazing Events and Astronomy Programs

Big Bend National Park is renowned for its breathtaking night skies, making it one of the best locations in the United States for stargazing and astronomical observations. With minimal light pollution, the park provides an exceptional opportunity to see stars, planets, and celestial events. This section explores the stargazing opportunities in Big Bend, including special events and astronomy programs.

Why Stargazing in Big Bend?

Dark Skies:

Big Bend is designated as a Dark Sky Park, meaning it has minimal artificial light and clear atmospheric conditions that allow for exceptional visibility of celestial bodies. Visitors can enjoy views of thousands of stars, the Milky Way galaxy, and various astronomical phenomena.

Celestial Events:

The park hosts several celestial events throughout the year, including meteor showers, planetary alignments, and lunar events. These events can make for unforgettable experiences, drawing visitors to the park to witness the beauty of the universe.

Stargazing Events

Star Parties:

Organized by the park rangers and local astronomy clubs, star parties are special events where visitors can join in for a night of stargazing. During these events, knowledgeable guides provide telescopes for public use, share insights about the night sky, and highlight various celestial objects.

>**When:**
>Star parties typically occur on weekends from spring to fall, depending on weather conditions and park schedules.

>**What to Expect:**
>Participants can expect to see planets like Jupiter and Saturn, star clusters, nebulae, and, on clear nights, the Milky Way. The rangers often provide educational talks about astronomy and tips for stargazing.

Meteor Showers:

Big Bend is an excellent location to witness meteor showers, such as the Perseids (August) and the Geminids (December). The park hosts viewing nights during these events, where rangers lead programs to educate visitors about the meteor shower and provide prime viewing spots.

Preparation:

For the best experience, find a location away from park buildings and road lights, and bring blankets or reclining chairs for comfortable viewing.

Lunar Events:

Special events are often held during full moons, allowing visitors to enjoy the unique perspective of the night sky illuminated by the moon. These events might include moonlit hikes or guided tours to learn about lunar phases and their impact on wildlife and the environment.

Astronomy Programs

Night Sky Programs:

Throughout the year, Big Bend offers educational programs focused on the night sky. These programs are designed for all ages and include presentations on constellations, celestial navigation, and the importance of dark skies.

Content:

Programs may feature multimedia presentations, interactive activities, and opportunities for hands-on learning. Participants can expect to gain a deeper understanding of the cosmos and its significance.

Guided Night Hikes:

Some ranger-led programs include night hikes, where visitors explore the park's trails under the stars. These hikes provide insights into nocturnal wildlife, the science of stargazing, and the cultural significance of celestial bodies.

What to Bring:

Participants should bring flashlights with red filters (to preserve night vision), water, and appropriate footwear for hiking.

Astronomy Workshops:

Occasionally, the park hosts workshops led by astronomers and astrophysicists. These workshops may cover topics such as astrophotography, telescope operation, and the physics of celestial objects.

Tips for Stargazing in Big Bend

Best Viewing Times:
The best times for stargazing are typically between late spring and early fall, when the skies are clearer and the weather is more favorable. New moon nights provide the darkest skies, enhancing visibility.

Bring the Right Gear:
While telescopes are provided during events, bringing your binoculars or a personal telescope can enhance your experience. A star map or stargazing app can help you identify celestial bodies.

Dress Appropriately:
Nights in the desert can be surprisingly cool, even in summer. Dress in layers and bring warm clothing, blankets, and camping chairs for comfort.

Stay Safe and Respect Nature:
Follow park guidelines to preserve the natural environment. Avoid using bright lights and stay on designated paths to minimize your impact.

Stargazing in Big Bend National Park is a magical experience that connects visitors with the vastness of the universe. With its dark skies and organized events, the park provides an excellent setting for enjoying the beauty of the night sky. Whether you join a star party, witness a meteor shower, or participate in educational programs, you'll leave with unforgettable memories and a deeper appreciation for the cosmos. Be sure to take advantage of these stargazing opportunities during your visit to Big Bend!

7. Visitor Services

7.1 Visitor Centers and Interpretive Programs

Big Bend National Park is not only a place of stunning natural beauty, but it also offers a range of visitor services designed to enhance your experience. One of the main attractions for visitors is the park's visitor centers and the various interpretive programs available. These services provide valuable information, educational opportunities, and resources to help you make the most of your visit. Here's a comprehensive overview of the visitor centers and interpretive programs in Big Bend.

Visitor Centers

Persimmon Gap Visitor Center

Location:
Near the northern entrance of the park, along Highway 385.

Hours of Operation:
Typically open from 8 AM to 5 PM, but hours may vary by season, so it's best to check the park's website for current information.

Facilities and Services:

Information Desk:
Friendly rangers and volunteers are available to answer questions, provide maps, and offer recommendations for hiking, camping, and scenic drives.

Exhibits:
The center features exhibits on the park's geology, flora, fauna, and cultural history, helping visitors gain a deeper understanding of the park's significance.

Restrooms:
Clean facilities are available for visitors.

Gift Shop:
A selection of books, maps, souvenirs, and educational materials are for sale, perfect for those looking to take a piece of Big Bend home with them.

Chisos Basin Visitor Center

Location:

Located in the heart of the Chisos Mountains, accessible via the road leading from the park entrance.

Hours of Operation:

Open from 8 AM to 5 PM, with seasonal variations.

Facilities and Services:

Information Desk:

Park staff are available to assist with questions, trail conditions, and safety tips for exploring the mountainous terrain.

Exhibits:

Learn about the unique ecosystems of the Chisos Mountains and the wildlife that inhabits this diverse area.

Restrooms:

Facilities are available for visitor convenience.

Café and Dining:

The nearby Chisos Mountains Lodge offers dining options where visitors can relax and enjoy a meal with scenic views.

Interpretive Programs

Big Bend National Park provides a variety of interpretive programs designed to enhance visitors' understanding and appreciation of the park's natural and cultural resources. These programs are led by knowledgeable rangers and volunteers who are passionate about sharing their love for the park.

Ranger-led Programs:

Nature Walks and Talks:

Join a ranger for guided hikes that explore the park's diverse ecosystems, geology, and history. These programs often focus on specific themes, such as desert plants, birdwatching, or the park's unique geology.

Evening Programs:

In the cooler months, rangers offer evening programs that cover a range of topics, from star gazing to wildlife presentations. These programs provide a chance to learn in a relaxed setting under the night sky.

Educational Workshops:

Workshops may be offered throughout the year on topics such as wildlife tracking, photography, or desert survival skills. These hands-on experiences are a great way to deepen your understanding of the park's environment.

Self-guided Programs:

For visitors who prefer to explore on their own, the visitor centers provide information on self-guided tours and interpretive trails. Many trails have signs along the way that explain the local flora and fauna, making it easy to learn as you hike.

Special Events:

Throughout the year, Big Bend hosts special events such as the "Big Bend Birding Festival" and "National Park Week" activities. These events often include guided hikes, workshops, and family-friendly programs.

Planning Your Visit to Visitor Services

Check the Schedule:

Before your visit, check the park's website for current hours of operation, program schedules, and any special events that may be taking place during your stay.

Visitor Center Amenities:

Be sure to take advantage of the amenities offered at the visitor centers, including maps, brochures, and ranger recommendations for activities that match your interests and abilities.

Engage with Staff:

Don't hesitate to ask park staff for advice or information about specific trails, wildlife sightings, or safety tips. They are knowledgeable and eager to help enhance your experience.

The visitor centers and interpretive programs at Big Bend National Park play a crucial role in enhancing your visit. They provide essential information, educational opportunities, and a deeper connection to the park's natural beauty and cultural history. Whether you're looking to learn more about the park's ecology, join a guided hike, or simply get advice on the best trails, the visitor services available will help you make the most of your Big Bend adventure.

7.2 Park Ranger Programs and Guided Tours

Big Bend National Park offers a variety of ranger-led programs and guided tours designed to enhance your experience in this stunning natural setting. These programs provide unique opportunities to learn about the park's ecology, history, and cultural significance while exploring its diverse landscapes. Here's a detailed look at the park ranger programs and guided tours available to visitors.

Park Ranger Programs

Guided Hikes

Overview:
Ranger-led hikes are an excellent way to explore the park's trails while learning about the local flora, fauna, geology, and history. Hikes vary in difficulty and duration, accommodating everyone from beginners to seasoned hikers.

What to Expect:
Rangers provide insights into the ecology of the park, sharing fascinating stories about the plants and animals you encounter along the way. Many hikes include stops at key points of interest, offering the chance to take photographs and enjoy breathtaking views.

Duration:
Hikes typically last from one to three hours, depending on the trail and group interest.

Evening Programs

Overview:
During the warmer months, rangers offer evening programs that often focus on the night sky, wildlife, and the unique sounds of the desert at night.

What to Expect:
These programs might include guided stargazing, storytelling around a campfire, or discussions about the park's nocturnal animals. Participants can learn how to identify constellations and planets visible in the park's dark skies.

Duration:

Evening programs usually last about an hour and can be held in various locations throughout the park.

Cultural and Historical Talks

Overview:

Rangers conduct presentations that delve into the cultural history of the area, discussing the indigenous peoples, early settlers, and the establishment of the national park.

What to Expect:

These talks often include artifacts, photographs, and stories that illustrate the rich cultural tapestry of Big Bend. Visitors can gain a deeper appreciation for the human history intertwined with the natural landscape.

Duration:

Presentations generally last around 30-60 minutes and can be offered at visitor centers or outdoor amphitheaters.

Junior Ranger Program

Overview:

This program is designed for children aged 5-12, encouraging young visitors to explore the park while learning about its natural and cultural resources.

What to Expect:

Kids can pick up a Junior Ranger booklet at any visitor center, completing fun activities as they explore the park. Once they finish the booklet, they can earn a Junior Ranger badge by participating in a ranger-led program or presenting their findings to a ranger.

Guided Tours

Van Tours

Overview:

Ranger-led van tours provide a comfortable way to explore the park, especially for those who may have difficulty hiking long distances. These tours cover significant landmarks and areas of interest within Big Bend.

What to Expect:

Participants will travel in a park van with a ranger who shares information about the park's history, geology, and ecology. Stops are often made at popular viewpoints and trailheads.

Duration:

Tours can last anywhere from 2 to 4 hours, depending on the route and group interests.

Backcountry Tours

Overview:

For the more adventurous, guided backcountry tours offer a chance to explore remote areas of the park. These tours may include hiking, camping, and exploring lesser-known trails.

What to Expect:

Rangers will lead the way through the rugged terrain, sharing insights about the park's ecosystems and helping participants connect with the natural world. These tours require a higher level of physical fitness and preparation.

Duration:

Backcountry tours can vary widely in duration, from half-day trips to multi-day excursions, depending on the group's experience and interest.

Wildlife Watching Tours

Overview:

Wildlife watching tours are led by rangers who are knowledgeable about the park's diverse animal species. These tours are ideal for those interested in observing and learning about the park's wildlife.

What to Expect:

Rangers will take participants to prime wildlife viewing locations and share tips on spotting animals. These tours may focus on specific wildlife, such as birds, mammals, or reptiles, depending on the season.

Duration:

Wildlife tours typically last around 2-3 hours and are scheduled during early morning or late afternoon when animals are most active.

Planning and Participation

Registration:
Many ranger-led programs and guided tours require advance registration, especially during peak seasons. Check the Big Bend National Park website or contact the visitor centers for details on how to sign up.

What to Bring:
When participating in ranger programs or guided tours, it's essential to wear comfortable clothing and sturdy shoes. Bring water, snacks, sunscreen, and binoculars (for wildlife watching) to enhance your experience.

Stay Informed:
Keep an eye on the park's event calendar for updates on scheduled ranger programs, as offerings can vary based on the season and weather conditions.

Park ranger programs and guided tours at Big Bend National Park offer visitors an incredible opportunity to explore the park's natural wonders and rich history. With knowledgeable rangers leading the way, you'll gain insights and experiences that will deepen your appreciation for this unique landscape. Whether you're hiking through the Chisos Mountains, gazing at the stars, or learning about the park's cultural heritage, these programs are a fantastic way to connect with the beauty and significance of Big Bend.

7.3 Accessibility Services and Resources

Big Bend National Park strives to make its natural beauty accessible to everyone, including individuals with disabilities. Understanding that accessibility can enhance the experience of all visitors, the park provides various services and resources to ensure everyone can enjoy its breathtaking landscapes and facilities. Here's a comprehensive overview of the accessibility services and resources available in Big Bend National Park.

General Accessibility Information

Visitor Centers:

Both the **Persimmon Gap Visitor Center** and **Chisos Basin Visitor Center** are equipped with accessible features, including:

Wheelchair-accessible entrances and restrooms.

Accessible parking spaces close to the entrances.

Informational materials available in alternative formats upon request.

Accessible Trails:

Big Bend offers a few accessible trails that allow visitors with mobility challenges to experience the park's stunning scenery. Notable trails include:

Chisos Basin Nature Trail:
This easy, 0.5-mile loop trail is mostly flat and paved, providing beautiful views of the surrounding mountains.

Santa Elena Canyon Trail:
A portion of this trail is accessible, leading to a scenic overlook of the canyon. The path may have some uneven surfaces but is manageable with assistance.

Transportation Services

Park Roads:

Most of the park's main roads are paved and offer scenic views that are accessible by car. Accessible parking is available at key locations throughout the park, including visitor centers and trailheads.

Shuttle Services:

While there are no public shuttle services operating within Big Bend, some private companies in nearby towns offer transportation options for those needing assistance. It's advisable to check for local services prior to your visit.

Facilities and Amenities

Restrooms:

Accessible restrooms are located at both visitor centers, campgrounds, and various picnic areas throughout the park. These facilities are designed to accommodate visitors with disabilities.

Camping:

The park provides accessible campsites at both **Rio Grande Village Campground** and **Chisos Basin Campground**. These sites include accessible picnic tables, fire rings, and restrooms nearby.

Interpretive Programs:

Many ranger-led programs can accommodate visitors with disabilities. Rangers are trained to adapt activities to ensure that everyone can participate. It's recommended to contact the park in advance to discuss specific needs or requests.

Visitor Assistance

Contacting the Park:

If you have specific questions about accessibility, it's best to contact the park directly before your visit. The staff can provide information about available resources, accommodations, and assistance options. You can reach the park at:

Phone: (432) 477-2251

Planning Ahead:

Visitors are encouraged to plan their trips in advance, considering any accessibility needs they may have. This includes looking up the latest information on trail conditions, program schedules, and any available assistance.

Assistance Animals:

Service animals are allowed in all public areas of the park. However, emotional support animals do not have the same access rights under the Americans with Disabilities Act (ADA).

Additional Resources

Accessibility Map:

Big Bend provides an accessibility map that highlights accessible facilities, trails, and viewpoints within the park. This resource can be obtained at visitor centers or downloaded from the park's website.

National Park Service Accessibility Resources:

The National Park Service has additional resources for visitors with disabilities, including guidelines on accessibility in national parks and tips for planning accessible trips. More information can be found on their official website.

Big Bend National Park is committed to providing an enjoyable and accessible experience for all visitors. With a range of services and resources tailored to individuals with disabilities, everyone can explore and appreciate the park's remarkable landscapes and rich natural heritage. If you have specific needs or questions, don't hesitate to reach out to the park staff for assistance. Planning ahead and utilizing the available resources will help ensure a memorable and enjoyable visit to Big Bend.

8. Local Culture and History

8.1 Indigenous Peoples and Their Heritage

The history of Big Bend National Park is deeply intertwined with the indigenous peoples who have called this region home for thousands of years. Understanding their heritage provides valuable insight into the cultural and historical significance of the area. This section explores the indigenous peoples of Big Bend, their traditions, and their enduring connection to the land.

The Indigenous Peoples of Big Bend

Groups Involved:

The area that is now Big Bend National Park has been inhabited by various indigenous tribes, including the **Chisos**, **Mescalero Apache**, and **Comanche**. Each of these groups has contributed to the rich cultural tapestry of the region.

Chisos People:

The Chisos people are believed to be one of the earliest inhabitants of the Big Bend region. They lived in the mountainous areas and relied on the diverse ecosystems for their subsistence, hunting game, and gathering wild plants.

Lifestyle:
The Chisos were semi-nomadic, moving with the seasons to take advantage of different resources. They built temporary shelters and used local materials for tools and crafts. Their connection to the land was profound, as they understood the rhythms of nature and the importance of sustainable living.

Mescalero Apache:

The Mescalero Apache migrated to the Big Bend region around the 17th century. They were skilled horsemen and hunters, known for their ability to navigate the rugged terrain of the mountains and canyons.

Cultural Practices:
The Mescalero Apache held deep spiritual beliefs connected to the land, emphasizing the importance of harmony with nature. They conducted ceremonies to honor their ancestors and sought guidance from the spirits in their daily lives.

Comanche Tribe:

The Comanche, known for their horse culture, traveled through the Big Bend area in pursuit of buffalo and other game. Their influence extended across large areas of Texas, and they were renowned for their fierce warrior spirit.

Impact on the Region:

The Comanche played a significant role in shaping the history of Texas through trade and conflict. Their presence in the region contributed to the rich history of the indigenous peoples in Big Bend.

Cultural Heritage and Traditions

Rock Art:

One of the most remarkable aspects of indigenous heritage in Big Bend is the presence of ancient rock art. The **Petroglyphs** and **pictographs** found in various locations throughout the park offer glimpses into the lives and beliefs of these early peoples.

Interpretation:

While the exact meanings of these images remain a mystery, they likely served as important cultural symbols, representing spiritual beliefs, hunting practices, and social stories.

Traditional Practices:

Indigenous peoples practiced a range of traditional skills, including weaving, pottery, and tool-making. These crafts were not only functional but also carried cultural significance, often passed down through generations.

Medicinal Knowledge:

Knowledge of local plants and their uses for medicine played a crucial role in the survival and health of indigenous communities. Many plants found in Big Bend have been used for centuries for their healing properties.

Language:

Indigenous languages, such as the **Chisos language**, were spoken in the region. Efforts are ongoing to preserve and revitalize these languages, reflecting the importance of cultural identity and heritage.

Modern-Day Indigenous Communities

Cultural Resilience:

Today, descendants of the original inhabitants of the Big Bend region continue to celebrate and preserve their cultural heritage. They participate in traditional ceremonies, share stories, and engage in efforts to educate others about their history.

Education and Awareness:

Local organizations and tribes work to raise awareness about the history and contributions of indigenous peoples. This includes hosting events, workshops, and educational programs in schools and communities.

Collaboration with National Parks:

Indigenous communities often collaborate with park officials to ensure that their cultural heritage is respected and integrated into the management of the land. This partnership fosters understanding and recognition of the indigenous peoples' connection to Big Bend.

The indigenous peoples of Big Bend National Park have a rich and diverse heritage that is deeply connected to the land. Their traditions, stories, and cultural practices have shaped the region's history and continue to influence the present. By acknowledging and respecting the legacy of the indigenous peoples, visitors to Big Bend can gain a deeper appreciation for the cultural significance of this remarkable landscape. Understanding their heritage not only enriches the experience of exploring the park but also honors the enduring connection that these communities have to the land.

8.2 Historical Sites within the Park

Big Bend National Park is not only a sanctuary for stunning natural landscapes but also a repository of rich history, with numerous historical sites that offer glimpses into the past. These sites reflect the diverse cultures, communities, and events that have shaped the region over centuries. Here's a comprehensive look at some significant historical sites within Big Bend National Park.

1. Castolon Historic District

Overview:
The Castolon Historic District is a former village that played a vital role in the area's history, particularly during the early 20th century. The site includes a collection of adobe buildings that were part of a small settlement and served as a trading post and agricultural community.

Significance:
Castolon was established in the 1900s by a group of settlers, including the influential **Dolan family**, who cultivated crops in the Rio Grande Valley. The district highlights the struggle of early settlers in adapting to the harsh desert environment.

Current Features:
Visitors can explore the restored buildings, which now house exhibits and artifacts related to the region's history. The **Castolon Visitor Center** offers information about the site and the broader history of the area.

2. The Old Maverick Road

Overview:
The Old Maverick Road is a historic unpaved road that runs through the park, once used by cattle drivers and early settlers as a route for moving livestock.

Significance:
Named after the famous Texas cattleman **Samuel Maverick**, this road reflects the ranching heritage of the region. It was a vital corridor for cattle drives in the 19th century and offers visitors a sense of the challenges faced by those who lived and worked in this remote area.

Current Features:
The road provides access to scenic vistas and unique geological formations. Along the way, visitors can find remnants of old ranches and other historical markers that tell the story of the area's ranching past.

3. Rio Grande Village

Overview:
Located along the banks of the Rio Grande, this area was historically significant as a point of trade and cultural exchange between Mexico and the United States.

Significance:
Rio Grande Village was a hub for early travelers and traders. It showcases the cultural interplay between the indigenous peoples, early settlers, and Mexican communities.

Current Features:
The village area features a developed campground and a visitor center that offers information on the historical significance of the region. The nearby **Hot Springs** are remnants of a historic bathhouse that once attracted visitors seeking relaxation and health benefits from the natural hot springs.

4. The Hot Springs Historic Site

Overview:
The Hot Springs site is famous for its natural hot springs, which have been used by indigenous peoples and later by settlers for their purported therapeutic benefits.

Significance:
The site was developed in the early 20th century as a resort destination. The remnants of the old bathhouse, built in 1908, provide insight into the early tourism in Big Bend.

Current Features:
Visitors can still enjoy the hot springs today, which flow at a temperature of about 105°F (40°C). The area features short walking trails leading to the historic bathhouse and offers stunning views of the Rio Grande and the surrounding landscapes.

5. The Sam Nail Ranch

Overview:
Located near the eastern entrance of the park, the Sam Nail Ranch offers a glimpse into the life of early 20th-century ranchers in the Big Bend region.

Significance:
The ranch was established in the 1920s by Sam Nail, who adapted to the harsh environment

by raising livestock and cultivating crops. It stands as a testament to the resilience and ingenuity of early settlers.

Current Features:
The ranch site includes the remains of the original buildings, which are now in ruins, and offers a walking trail that provides interpretive signage about the history of ranching in Big Bend. Visitors can explore the area while enjoying the scenic views of the surrounding landscape.

6. The Historic Chisos Basin Lodge

Overview:
The Chisos Basin Lodge, built in the 1960s, is an important historical landmark within the park. It was designed to blend with the natural environment while providing comfortable accommodations for visitors.

Significance:
The lodge has served as a base for countless adventurers exploring the Chisos Mountains. Its architecture reflects the mid-century modern style that emphasizes harmony with the landscape.

Current Features:
The lodge offers lodging and dining options, making it a convenient spot for visitors. The surrounding area features hiking trails and stunning vistas, encouraging guests to immerse themselves in the natural beauty of Big Bend.

Big Bend National Park is rich in history, with numerous sites that showcase the cultural heritage and historical significance of the region. From ancient indigenous peoples to early settlers and ranchers, the stories embedded in these historical sites provide visitors with a deeper understanding of the land and its people. Exploring these sites not only enhances your experience in the park but also allows you to appreciate the resilience and spirit of those who have come before us. As you wander through Big Bend, take the time to reflect on the history that has shaped this remarkable landscape.

8.3 Local Art and Cultural Events

Big Bend National Park is not only a natural wonder but also a vibrant cultural hub that celebrates the rich heritage of the region through art, music, and various cultural events. The local community and artists contribute to this lively atmosphere, offering visitors a unique glimpse into the artistic expressions and traditions that thrive in and around the park. Here's a comprehensive overview of the local art scene and cultural events in the Big Bend area.

1. Local Art Scene

Artists and Artisans:

The Big Bend region is home to many talented artists and artisans who draw inspiration from the stunning landscapes, wildlife, and cultural history of the area. Their work often reflects the natural beauty and unique characteristics of the desert environment.

Types of Art:
Local artists produce a wide range of art forms, including painting, sculpture, photography, pottery, and textile arts. Many of these creations can be found in local galleries, shops, and art fairs.

Art Galleries:

Several galleries in nearby towns, such as **Marfa**, **Alpine**, and **Terlingua**, showcase the work of local artists. Notable galleries include:

The Chinati Foundation (Marfa): A contemporary art museum founded by artist Donald Judd, featuring large-scale installations and works by various artists.

Marfa Book Company (Marfa): A bookstore and gallery that often hosts exhibitions and events focusing on literary and visual arts.

Big Bend Arts & Crafts (Alpine): A cooperative gallery showcasing handmade crafts and art from local artisans.

Public Art Installations:

Public art can be found throughout the region, with various sculptures and installations enhancing the outdoor spaces. These artworks often reflect the cultural heritage and natural environment of Big Bend.

2. Cultural Events

Annual Events:

The Big Bend area hosts several annual events that celebrate local culture, art, and traditions. Some notable events include:

Marfa Lights Festival: Celebrated every spring, this festival honors the mysterious lights that appear near Marfa. The event features music, art, and local food, bringing together residents and visitors for a night of fun and exploration.

Chinati Weekend (Marfa): Held in the fall, this event includes guided tours of the Chinati Foundation, art talks, and performances, showcasing the vibrant art scene in Marfa.

Terlingua Chili Cook-Off: This lively event attracts chili enthusiasts and food lovers from all over, featuring a weekend of chili tasting, live music, and family-friendly activities.

Cultural Festivals:

Various cultural festivals throughout the year highlight the diverse heritage of the region, including:

Fiesta de la Candelaria (Terlingua): Celebrated in early February, this festival includes music, dance, and traditional food, honoring the local Hispanic culture and community.

Alpine Artwalk: This event takes place in April and features a gallery walk showcasing local artists, live music, and food vendors, promoting the creative spirit of Alpine.

Live Music and Performances:

The Big Bend region is known for its lively music scene, with local venues hosting performances by regional and traveling artists. Common music genres include country, folk, and rock, often reflecting the local culture and traditions.

The Starlight Theatre in Terlingua: A popular venue offering live music and performances, it often features local talent and serves as a gathering place for the community.

3. Workshops and Classes

Art Workshops:

> Many local artists and organizations offer workshops and classes for those interested in learning new skills or exploring their creativity. These workshops often focus on specific mediums, such as painting, pottery, or photography, and are suitable for all skill levels.

Cultural Workshops:

> Cultural events and workshops provide opportunities for visitors to engage with local traditions. These may include cooking classes focused on traditional Tex-Mex cuisine, storytelling sessions, or craft workshops where participants can learn about local artisanship.

The local art and cultural events in the Big Bend region create a vibrant tapestry that enhances the overall experience of visiting the park. From the breathtaking artworks inspired by the stunning landscapes to the lively festivals celebrating the rich heritage of the area, there is something for everyone to enjoy. Engaging with the local culture not only enriches your visit but also supports the artists and communities that call Big Bend home. Whether you're exploring galleries, attending a festival, or participating in a workshop, you'll discover that the spirit of creativity and tradition is alive and well in this remarkable part of Texas.

9. Dining and Shopping

9.1 Restaurants and Cafés Near the Park

When visiting Big Bend National Park, it's essential to fuel up with delicious meals and snacks, whether you're preparing for a day of adventure or unwinding after exploring the stunning landscapes. Here's a guide to some of the best restaurants and cafés near the park, complete with addresses, contact information, and price ranges to help you plan your dining experience.

The Starlight Theatre Restaurant & Saloon

Address: 209 Starlight Ave, Terlingua, TX 79852

Contact: (432) 371-3382

Price Range: $15 - $30

Overview:
This iconic venue offers a lively atmosphere with a menu featuring Tex-Mex favorites and American classics. You can enjoy dishes like fajitas, burgers, and tacos, accompanied by live music in the evenings. The Starlight Theatre is famous for its outdoor seating area, providing stunning views of the desert landscape.

Chisos Mountains Lodge Restaurant

Address: 402 Chisos Basin Rd, Big Bend National Park, TX 79834

Contact: (432) 477-2291

Price Range: $10 - $25

Overview:
Located within Big Bend National Park, this lodge restaurant serves breakfast, lunch, and dinner, featuring a selection of hearty meals made from locally sourced ingredients. The menu includes sandwiches, salads, and daily specials, along with a

beautiful view of the surrounding mountains. Reservations are recommended during peak seasons.

The 11th Street Cowboy Bar

Address: 11th St, Bandera, TX 78003 (Note: The name can be confusing, as this bar is actually in Bandera, TX, but it's well-known in the area)

Contact: (830) 796-4828

Price Range: $10 - $20

Overview:
A popular spot for both locals and visitors, this cowboy bar offers a casual dining experience with a menu featuring burgers, sandwiches, and appetizers. The lively atmosphere includes live music and dancing, making it a fun place to unwind after a day of exploring.

La Kiva

Address: 1351 Terlingua Ranch Rd, Terlingua, TX 79852

Contact: (432) 371-3044

Price Range: $10 - $20

Overview:
Nestled in a cave-like setting, La Kiva is a unique restaurant known for its laid-back vibe. The menu features a variety of Tex-Mex dishes, burgers, and daily specials. Their outdoor seating area is perfect for enjoying a meal under the stars.

Pueblo Viejo

Address: 802 W. Main St, Alpine, TX 79830

Contact: (432) 837-1134

Price Range: $10 - $20

Overview:
Located about an hour from Big Bend, Pueblo Viejo offers a delightful menu featuring authentic Mexican cuisine, including enchiladas, tacos, and tamales. The

restaurant is known for its friendly service and cozy atmosphere, making it a great stop for lunch or dinner.

Big Bend Coffee Roasters

Address: 300 Farm to Market Rd 170, Terlingua, TX 79852

Contact: (432) 371-2630

Price Range: $5 - $10

Overview:
This café specializes in artisanal coffee roasted on-site. It's the perfect spot to grab a quick breakfast or a refreshing beverage before heading into the park. In addition to coffee, they offer pastries and light breakfast options, all served in a relaxed setting.

The Alpine Rose Restaurant

Address: 1601 S. 5th St, Alpine, TX 79830

Contact: (432) 837-6700

Price Range: $10 - $25

Overview:
Located in Alpine, this charming restaurant offers a variety of dishes, including steaks, seafood, and vegetarian options. The warm ambiance and friendly service make it a favorite for both locals and visitors. Reservations are recommended during busy seasons.

The Lost Horse Saloon

Address: 18000 Farm to Market Rd 170, Terlingua, TX 79852

Contact: (432) 371-2140

Price Range: $10 - $20

Overview:
A local favorite, the Lost Horse Saloon serves classic American bar food with a Southwestern twist. Enjoy a laid-back atmosphere with burgers, wings.

Dining options near Big Bend National Park range from casual cafés to more formal restaurants, offering a variety of flavors and atmospheres to suit every palate. Whether you're craving hearty Tex-Mex, delicious coffee, or a refreshing drink after a day of exploring, the local dining scene has something for everyone. Be sure to check hours of operation and availability, especially during peak tourist seasons, to ensure a delightful dining experience during your visit to Big Bend.

9.2 Local Food Specialties

The Big Bend region of Texas is rich in culinary traditions, influenced by its diverse cultural heritage and the abundance of local ingredients. When visiting the area, you'll encounter several local food specialties that reflect the unique flavors and traditions of this remarkable landscape. Here's a comprehensive overview of some must-try local dishes and food items during your visit.

Tex-Mex Cuisine

Overview:
A fusion of Texas and Mexican culinary traditions, Tex-Mex is a staple in the Big Bend area. Dishes often feature ingredients such as cheese, tortillas, beans, and various meats.

Must-Try Dishes:

Tacos: Soft or crispy tortillas filled with various ingredients, including beef, chicken, pork, and vegetables. Look for unique local variations, such as breakfast tacos with eggs and chorizo.

Enchiladas: Rolled tortillas filled with meat or cheese, topped with chili sauce and melted cheese.

Chili con Carne: A spicy stew made with ground beef, chili peppers, and spices. Some local eateries offer their unique versions with additional ingredients like beans or tomatoes.

Local Barbecue

Overview:

Texas is famous for its barbecue, and the Big Bend area is no exception. Local barbecue often features slow-cooked meats, smoky flavors, and delicious sides.

Must-Try Items:

Brisket: Tender, slow-cooked beef brisket, often served with a side of barbecue sauce and pickles.

Ribs: Pork or beef ribs smoked to perfection, typically served with sides like coleslaw and baked beans.

Sausage: Many barbecue joints offer house-made sausages, which are often smoked and packed with flavor.

Nopalitos

Overview:

Nopalitos are young cactus pads that are commonly used in Mexican cuisine. They have a slightly tangy flavor and a unique texture.

How to Enjoy:

Nopalitos can be grilled, sautéed, or added to salads and tacos. Look for dishes featuring nopalitos at local restaurants, especially those specializing in traditional Mexican food.

Chili Peppers

Overview:

The Big Bend region is known for its spicy chili peppers, which are often incorporated into various dishes, adding heat and flavor.

Must-Try Varieties:

Jalapeños: Popular for their moderate heat, jalapeños are often used in salsas, stuffed dishes, or grilled.

Anaheim Peppers: Mild and sweet, these peppers are great for roasting or stuffing.

Hatch Green Chiles: Renowned for their flavor, Hatch chiles are available in various dishes and can be found fresh in season.

Mesquite-Grilled Dishes

Overview:
Mesquite wood is commonly used for grilling in the Big Bend area, imparting a distinct smoky flavor to meats and vegetables.

Must-Try Items:

Mesquite-Grilled Steak: Tender cuts of beef grilled over mesquite, often seasoned simply with salt and pepper.

Vegetables: Local restaurants often offer grilled vegetables, such as zucchini, bell peppers, and onions, as delicious side options.

Homemade Desserts

Overview:
Sweet treats are a highlight of dining in the Big Bend region, with many local establishments serving homemade desserts.

Must-Try Desserts:

Pan de Campo: A traditional cowboy bread that is often served warm and can be enjoyed with butter or jam.

Cobbler: Seasonal fruit cobblers made with local fruits like peaches or berries, served with ice cream or whipped cream.

Tres Leches Cake: A moist cake soaked in three types of milk, often topped with whipped cream and fresh fruit.

The local food specialties in the Big Bend region offer a delightful exploration of flavors and culinary traditions. Whether you're indulging in hearty Tex-Mex, savoring smoked barbecue, or enjoying fresh local produce, the area's unique dishes are sure to satisfy your taste buds. Don't miss the opportunity to experience these delicious offerings during your visit to Big Bend National Park.

9.3 Gift Shops and Local Artisans

In addition to enjoying the natural beauty of Big Bend National Park, visitors can also explore local shops that feature unique gifts, artisan crafts, and souvenirs. Here's a guide to some of the best gift shops and local artisans in the area, where you can find one-of-a-kind items to take home.

Big Bend National Park Visitor Center Gift Shop

Location: Panther Junction, Big Bend National Park, TX 79834

Overview:
This gift shop offers a variety of park-related merchandise, including maps, books, and souvenirs. You'll find clothing, hats, and educational materials that celebrate the park's natural wonders and wildlife.

The Terlingua Trading Company

Address: 1000 W. Terlingua Ranch Rd, Terlingua, TX 79852

Contact: (432) 371-2200

Overview:
A local favorite, this trading company offers a wide range of unique gifts, including Native American crafts, home décor, jewelry, and local art. It's an excellent place to find special keepsakes that reflect the region's culture.

Alpine Gift Shop

Address: 1400 W. Highway 90, Alpine, TX 79830

Contact: (432) 837-7111

Overview:
Located in nearby Alpine, this shop features an eclectic mix of items, including local art, crafts, souvenirs, and regional food products. Visitors can find handmade pottery, textiles, and other artisan goods created by local artists.

La Kiva Art Gallery

Address: 1351 Terlingua Ranch Rd, Terlingua, TX 79852

Overview:
This gallery showcases the work of local artists, including paintings, sculptures, and mixed-media pieces. It's an excellent place to discover unique art that captures the essence of the Big Bend landscape.

Coyote Coyote

Address: 200 E. Main St, Terlingua, TX 79852

Overview:
A quirky gift shop offering a range of whimsical and eclectic items, from handmade crafts to unusual home décor. It's a fun stop to find unique gifts that reflect the spirit of Terlingua.

Lost Horse Saloon Gift Shop

Address: 18000 Farm to Market Rd 170, Terlingua, TX 79852

Contact: (432) 371-2140

Overview:
The Lost Horse Saloon has a small gift shop featuring T-shirts, hats, and local art. It's a great place to pick up a memento of your visit while enjoying the lively atmosphere of the saloon.

Marfa Book Company

Address: 105 S. Highland Ave, Marfa, TX 79843

Contact: (432) 729-2300

Overview:
A unique bookstore that also features art and cultural items, the Marfa Book Company is a great spot to find books on regional history, art, and photography. They often host events and exhibitions featuring local artists.

Art Galleries in Marfa

Overview:
Marfa is known for its vibrant arts scene, with numerous galleries showcasing contemporary and traditional art. Visit places like **Planet Marfa** and **The Chinati Foundation** for art exhibitions and opportunities to purchase original works from local artists.

Conclusion

Exploring the local gift shops and artisans in the Big Bend region offers a wonderful way to find unique souvenirs and support the local economy. From handcrafted items to regional art, the shops around Big Bend National Park provide a glimpse into the creative spirit of the area. Whether you're searching for the perfect memento of your trip or a special gift for someone back home, the local offerings will surely inspire you.

10. Sustainability and Conservation

As a visitor to Big Bend National Park, it's essential to understand the importance of sustainability and conservation efforts that help preserve this beautiful landscape for future generations. This section will provide insights into the Leave No Trace principles, the park's conservation initiatives, and how you, as a visitor, can contribute to preserving the natural beauty of Big Bend.

10.1 Leave No Trace Principles

The Leave No Trace principles are guidelines designed to help outdoor enthusiasts minimize their impact on the environment. By following these principles, you can ensure that the natural beauty of Big Bend National Park is preserved. Here are the seven core principles:

Plan Ahead and Prepare

Research the park before your visit, including trail conditions, weather forecasts, and regulations. Being well-prepared helps you stay safe and reduce your impact on the environment.

Travel and Camp on Durable Surfaces

Stick to established trails and campsites to prevent soil erosion and damage to vegetation. Avoid creating new trails or campsites in sensitive areas.

Dispose of Waste Properly

Pack out all trash, leftover food, and personal items. Use designated restroom facilities when available. If you're in a backcountry area, bury human waste at least six inches deep, away from water sources.

Leave What You Find

Preserve the natural and cultural resources of the park by not removing rocks, plants, or artifacts. Enjoy the scenery without disturbing it.

Minimize Campfire Impact

Use a stove for cooking instead of a campfire when possible. If fires are permitted, use established fire rings and keep them small. Always collect firewood from the ground and never cut live trees or branches.

Respect Wildlife

Observe animals from a distance, and do not feed or approach them. Keep your food secure to avoid attracting wildlife to your campsite.

Be Considerate of Other Visitors

Keep noise levels down and be respectful of other park-goers. Yield the trail to others, especially those on foot and those with animals.

10.2 Park Conservation Efforts

Big Bend National Park has implemented several conservation efforts to protect its unique ecosystems and cultural heritage. Here are some key initiatives:

Wildlife Protection

The park conducts monitoring programs for various wildlife species, including endangered species like the Texas horned lizard. Efforts are made to maintain habitats and manage invasive species to support biodiversity.

Restoration Projects

Restoration projects are undertaken to rehabilitate disturbed areas, such as trails and campsites. The park works to re-establish native vegetation and improve habitats for local wildlife.

Water Conservation

With water being a precious resource in the Chihuahuan Desert, the park implements water conservation practices and educates visitors on the importance of water sustainability.

Cultural Resource Management

The park is home to numerous archaeological sites and historic structures. Conservation efforts focus on preserving these cultural resources for future generations, including regular assessments and restoration work.

Visitor Education

Park staff engage in educational outreach to inform visitors about the importance of conservation and sustainable practices. Programs and workshops are offered to encourage responsible park use.

10.3 How Visitors Can Help

Visitors play a crucial role in the conservation of Big Bend National Park. Here are some ways you can contribute:

Educate Yourself and Others

Learn about the park's ecosystems, wildlife, and cultural history. Share this knowledge with fellow visitors to raise awareness about conservation efforts.

Follow Leave No Trace Principles

Adhere to the Leave No Trace principles during your visit to minimize your impact on the park's natural resources.

Participate in Volunteer Programs

Check with park staff about volunteer opportunities, such as trail maintenance, clean-up events, and educational outreach programs.

Support Local Conservation Organizations

Consider donating to or volunteering with organizations dedicated to preserving the natural beauty of Big Bend and its surrounding areas.

Report Issues

If you encounter any issues such as litter, damaged trails, or distressed wildlife, report them to park staff. Your observations can help park rangers address problems quickly.

Choose Sustainable Practices

Use refillable water bottles, choose eco-friendly products, and be mindful of your energy consumption while visiting. Support businesses that prioritize sustainability.

Respect Wildlife Regulations

Follow all park regulations regarding wildlife viewing and behavior. This helps protect both the animals and their habitats.

Sustainability and conservation are essential components of enjoying and preserving Big Bend National Park. By understanding and applying the Leave No Trace principles, supporting conservation efforts, and taking an active role in protecting the environment, you can contribute to the ongoing health and beauty of this incredible landscape. Together, we can ensure that future generations will have the opportunity to experience the wonders of Big Bend National Park.

11. Frequently Asked Questions

When planning a trip to Big Bend National Park, many visitors have questions about what to expect and how to make the most of their experience. This section addresses common visitor concerns and provides tips for first-time visitors to help ensure a safe and enjoyable adventure.

11.1 Common Visitor Concerns

What are the park hours?

Big Bend National Park is open 24 hours a day, year-round. However, visitor centers and some facilities may have limited hours, especially during the off-peak season. Always check the park's official website for the latest information.

Is there cell phone reception in the park?

Cell phone reception can be spotty throughout the park. Many areas, especially remote hiking trails and backcountry sites, have little to no signal. It's best to inform someone of your plans and carry a physical map.

Are there restroom facilities in the park?

Yes, restroom facilities are available at key locations, including visitor centers and campgrounds. However, in the backcountry, there may not be any facilities, so be prepared to follow proper waste disposal practices.

What should I do in case of an emergency?

In case of an emergency, dial 911 for assistance. It's important to be familiar with your surroundings and know the location of the nearest visitor center or ranger station. Carry a first aid kit and let someone know your plans before heading out.

Can I bring my pet to the park?

Pets are allowed in designated areas, including campgrounds and along paved roads. However, they are not permitted on hiking trails or in backcountry areas. Always keep pets on a leash and clean up after them.

What is the weather like in Big Bend?

The weather can vary significantly depending on the season. Summers can be extremely hot, with temperatures exceeding 100°F (38°C), while winters can be chilly, especially at night. Always check the forecast before your visit and pack accordingly.

Is there food available in the park?

Dining options within the park are limited. The Chisos Mountains Lodge offers a restaurant and café, but outside of that, visitors should plan to bring their own food and supplies. Grocery stores and restaurants are available in nearby towns like Terlingua and Alpine.

Are there any fees to enter the park?

Yes, there is an entrance fee for Big Bend National Park. As of 2024, the fee is $30 per vehicle for a seven-day pass. Check the park's website for updated fee information and any available discounts.

11.2 Tips for First-Time Visitors

Plan Ahead

Research the park before your visit, including maps, trail conditions, and areas of interest. Having a plan will help you make the most of your time in the park.

Stay Hydrated

The desert climate can lead to dehydration quickly. Carry plenty of water and drink regularly, especially during hikes or strenuous activities.

Start Early

To avoid the heat and crowds, consider starting your day early. Morning hikes often offer cooler temperatures and the chance to see wildlife.

Wear Appropriate Footwear

Good hiking shoes or boots are essential for exploring the park's varied terrain. Make sure they are comfortable and broken in to prevent blisters.

Layer Your Clothing

Due to temperature fluctuations, especially in the mountains, wear layers that can be easily added or removed. Lightweight, moisture-wicking clothing is ideal for outdoor activities.

Bring a Map and Compass

While GPS can be helpful, it may not always work in remote areas. A physical map and compass are reliable tools to navigate the park.

Respect Wildlife

Observe animals from a safe distance and never feed them. Remember that wildlife is wild and can be unpredictable.

Check Trail Conditions

Before heading out, check trail conditions at visitor centers or on the park's website. Some trails may be closed or have specific guidelines due to weather or maintenance.

Engage with Park Rangers

Don't hesitate to ask park rangers for recommendations or information. They can provide valuable insights and help you enhance your experience.

Take Your Time

Allow yourself to enjoy the scenery and take breaks. Big Bend's beauty is best appreciated at a leisurely pace, so don't rush through your visit.

Conclusion

By being informed about common visitor concerns and following these tips, first-time visitors can navigate Big Bend National Park with confidence. Embrace the adventure, and take the time to soak in the stunning landscapes, diverse wildlife, and rich history that make this park truly special. Enjoy your trip!

12. Resources

Planning a visit to Big Bend National Park is exciting, and having the right resources can make your experience smoother and more enjoyable. This section provides useful websites and apps for park information and planning, as well as essential emergency contacts for your safety.

12.1 Useful Websites and Apps

National Park Service (NPS) – Big Bend National Park

Website: nps.gov/bibe

The official website offers comprehensive information about the park, including hours of operation, entrance fees, maps, trail conditions, visitor services, and current events. It's a great starting point for planning your visit.

Big Bend National Park App

Available On: iOS and Android

This mobile app provides valuable information about the park, including maps, trail details, points of interest, and upcoming ranger programs. It works offline, which is handy in areas with limited cell service.

AllTrails

Website: https://www.alltrails.com

An excellent resource for finding detailed trail maps, reviews, and photos. You can filter trails by difficulty, length, and user ratings to find the perfect hike for your skill level.

Weather Underground

Website: https://www.wunderground.com

For accurate weather forecasts and conditions specific to Big Bend National Park, this site provides real-time updates. Knowing the weather can help you plan your daily activities effectively.

ParkFinder

Website: nps.gov/findapark

Use this site to discover other national parks and find travel tips, itineraries, and helpful information about various destinations in the National Park System.

TripAdvisor

Website: https://www.tripadvisor.com

This travel review site provides insights from other visitors, including accommodation reviews, dining recommendations, and things to do in and around Big Bend.

Local Guides and Maps

Many local gas stations and visitor centers offer paper maps and brochures highlighting the best places to visit, eat, and stay. Don't hesitate to pick these up for additional information.

12.2 Emergency Contacts

While Big Bend National Park is generally safe for visitors, it's essential to be prepared for emergencies. Here are key emergency contacts and resources:

Park Emergency (Law Enforcement, Medical, and Fire)

Phone Number: 911

In case of an emergency, dial 911 for immediate assistance. This number can be used for any law enforcement, medical, or fire emergencies within the park.

Big Bend National Park Headquarters

Phone Number: (432) 477-2251

The park headquarters can provide assistance and information about park regulations, services, and emergency situations.

Visitor Centers

Chisos Basin Visitor Center

Phone Number: (432) 477-2641

Open year-round, this center provides maps, information on trails, and advice from park rangers.

Persimmon Gap Visitor Center

Phone Number: (432) 477-2272

This center is located near the park entrance and offers resources for first-time visitors.

Texas Parks and Wildlife Department

Phone Number: (512) 389-4800

For issues related to wildlife or fishing regulations, you can contact the Texas Parks and Wildlife Department for guidance.

Terlingua Fire Department

Phone Number: (432) 371-2101

The local fire department can provide emergency services if needed in nearby areas.

Health and Medical Services

Big Bend Regional Medical Center (in Alpine)

Address: 805 E. Sul Ross Ave, Alpine, TX 79830

Phone Number: (432) 837-7100

This facility is the nearest full-service hospital and can provide emergency medical care if needed.

Conclusion

Having access to the right resources and knowing where to turn in case of an emergency can significantly enhance your experience at Big Bend National Park. With the help of websites, apps, and essential contacts, you can explore this stunning park with confidence and ease. Safe travels!

13. Conclusion

As you wrap up your travel plans for Big Bend National Park, it's essential to reflect on the adventure that awaits you. This park is a treasure trove of natural beauty, cultural history, and recreational opportunities, offering a unique experience for every visitor.

13.1 Final Thoughts and Encouragement to Explore Big Bend

Big Bend National Park is unlike any other destination. Its vast landscapes stretch across mountains, deserts, and rivers, creating an awe-inspiring backdrop for exploration and adventure. Whether you're hiking rugged trails, camping under a blanket of stars, or simply soaking in the breathtaking vistas, every moment spent in the park is an opportunity to connect with nature.

As you venture into the park, remember to embrace the spirit of exploration. Take your time to discover hidden gems, engage with park rangers for insights, and immerse yourself in the stunning scenery. Don't be afraid to step off the beaten path—some of the most rewarding experiences can be found in the quieter corners of the park.

Big Bend is not just a destination; it's a place that invites you to slow down and appreciate the natural world. From the rich tapestry of flora and fauna to the deep cultural heritage of the region, every aspect of the park tells a story waiting to be uncovered. Take the opportunity to learn about the Indigenous peoples who have called this land home for centuries and to appreciate the unique ecosystems that thrive in such an arid environment.

Whether you're a seasoned adventurer or visiting for the first time, Big Bend National Park offers something for everyone. The rugged beauty and serene isolation provide a perfect escape from the hustle and bustle of everyday life. So pack your bags, prepare for adventure, and set out to create lasting memories in this incredible national park.

In closing, remember that every visit contributes to the ongoing conservation efforts that protect this precious landscape. By respecting the park's resources and adhering to the principles of sustainability, you help ensure that Big Bend remains a haven for future generations.

So go ahead—explore, discover, and enjoy all that Big Bend National Park has to offer. Your adventure awaits!

Acknowledgments

Creating this travel guide for Big Bend National Park would not have been possible without the contributions and support of many individuals and organizations.

First and foremost, I would like to express my gratitude to the **National Park Service** for their dedication to preserving the natural beauty and cultural heritage of Big Bend. Their extensive resources and commitment to education have been invaluable in compiling accurate and up-to-date information.

Special thanks to the **park rangers** and staff, whose passion for the park and its history shines through in their work. Their insights and recommendations have helped shape a comprehensive guide that captures the essence of Big Bend.

I also want to acknowledge the countless **travelers and outdoor enthusiasts** who have shared their experiences, tips, and photographs online. Their stories and advice have provided inspiration and practical guidance that enhance this guide.

Additionally, I am grateful to the local businesses and communities surrounding Big Bend, particularly those in **Terlingua and Alpine**. Their hospitality and unique offerings enrich the visitor experience and play a vital role in supporting conservation efforts.

Finally, a heartfelt thank you to family and friends for their encouragement and support throughout the writing process. Their enthusiasm for exploring national parks has been a constant source of motivation.

As you embark on your journey to Big Bend National Park, may you be inspired by the beauty of nature and the rich history that this remarkable place offers. Thank you for taking the time to explore and appreciate one of America's most treasured landscapes. Happy travels!

Made in the USA
Coppell, TX
30 November 2024